USEFUL TOIL AND HOMELY JOYS

To: Deanne, Peter + Christopher
from Mum + Dad.

8 OCTOBER 2000.

Horningsham from the Church.

Useful Toil *and* Homely Joys

A Photographic Record of Horningsham and Longleat

Helen Taylor

Helen Taylor
1/10/00

ELSP

Published in 2000 by
ELSP
1 The Shambles
Bradford on Avon
Wiltshire
BA15 1JS

Design and typesetting by
Ex Libris Press

Printed in England by
Cromwell Press
Trowbridge
Wiltshire

ISBN 1 903341 56 6

CONTENTS

Acknowledgements

The seeds for this book were sown in 1994. Horningsham Church was approaching its 150th year since re-building, and I was keen to celebrate this in some way. On the first Sunday in October the theme of our village service was the church's 'birthday' and it was a great success. The following year we held the first of our annual reunions, the themes being Christening, Marriage, In Memoriam, the School and the Village Fair. Central to the occasion has been a display of photographs which people were kind enough to lend me each year. At the School reunion someone suggested I put them all in a book; two years later this is the result.

Although there is only one name on the cover, many people have contributed to this book. I would especially like to thank Vera Crossman for her unfailing energy and enthusiasm, and for her willingness to share her vast collection of pictures and her memories and local knowledge; Michael Marshman, the County Local Studies Librarian, for his advice, support and encouragement over the last year; Jack Field and Alwyn Hardy for their friendship, help and support on a daily basis; Sydney Battson, Connie Bull, Barbara Carpenter, Harold Howlett, Albert Honey, Maurice and Evelyn Robertson and Dorothy Russell, who not only lent me photographs but shared their memories and answered numerous questions; Dr. Kate Harris, who was able to answer many questions about Longleat; the late Miss Anderson, whose class photographs formed the core of my first display; John Radley, whose idea this book was; finally, thank you to my parents Gordon and Leonie Taylor for their unfailing support. David Burnett's book 'Longleat' was extremely useful, as were the *Warminster Journal* and the Trail around Horningsham written by the Womens Institute.

I am also very grateful to the following for lending me their photographs. The Marquess of Bath, who allowed me to use material from the Longleat House collection, Valerie Adams, Derek Bayes, Monica Booker, David Carpenter, Frances Chris, Peter Clark, County Local Studies Library, County Record Office, Carol Cox, James Crees, Paddy and Sheila Dalton, Dewey Museum, Mary Dix, Ken and Muriel Doel, Bert Dredge, Ann Dufosee, Michael and the late Nicola Evans, Marjorie Fennessy, the late Mary Ford, Rodney Garton, Doris Harding, Dorothy and the late Ivan Haskell, Suzanne Hill, Tim Hill, Gillian House, Sue Ivey, Canon Anthony Johnson, John McHardy, Alan Marsh, Victor and Eileen Marsh, Ray and Olive New, Islay Peet, Monty Penny Snr, Monty Penny Jnr, Martin Pring, Bernard Russell, Canon Roger Sharpe, Ray Shorto, Pamela Stay, the Rev. Alison Wadsworth, Western Daily Press, John Whatley, the late Les Wheeler, Valerie Wheeler, Susan Woodey and Edna Young.

The information contained in this book is, to the best of my knowledge, correct. If there are any errors, I would welcome corrections.

Foreword

Horningsham is a beautiful village, and I feel privileged to have grown up there. I have always been interested in its history. As a child I went with my father to 'help' mow the churchyard, but spent more time reading the gravestones than trimming round them! At school we were taken on walks around the village and given an idea of our community's past industries. When I left school and went to work for the Library Service I discovered Sir Richard Colt Hoare's *Modern History of Wiltshire*, and this inspired me to start my research.

The village has changed dramatically since the War - not in appearance, but the people who live there. There are few people in the village who were actually born there, and those who can remember what it was like sixty or more years ago are scattered the length and breadth of the country. The dawn of a new millennium seemed a good time to capture in print a way of life that would otherwise be lost forever.

Since starting our reunions and having had the opportunity to talk to some of you, I have been impressed by three things. Firstly, that Horningsham remained self-sufficient until the War. In the early 1930s there were numerous farms, and all the cottage industries, shops and small businesses that the community needed to keep it running. Secondly, that everyone knew how to enjoy themselves! Football, Cricket, Bowls, Mothers Union, Womens Guild, Womens Institute, Reading Room, Flower Show and a Youth Club all flourished. Finally, that so many people have fond memories of Horningsham and enjoy coming back. I hope they all feel proud to have been part of such a thriving community, and also proud to have contributed to this book. May you all enjoy looking through it as much as I have enjoyed compiling it.

Horningsham.— Stands in the midst of a most picturesque district. Bishop Ken used to attend the Church whilst he was a guest at Longleat. Horningsham possesses an old dissenting Chapel dated 1569.

Views and Houses

The scattered parish of Horningsham was originally created out of Selwood forest. It has an entry in Domesday, but was very small. Along with Corsley, Horningsham amounted to just one hide of land (c. 120 acres) and was occupied by one cottager and four smallholders. Its value was just 15s. Comparison with surrounding villages shows that Horningsham was one of the smallest and poorest communities. Hoare, however, disputes this. It was his opinion that either the Canons who owned the land were favoured by making the value less than it really was, or that the pasture land was not worth including.

The church was built in 1154 by the Vernon family, who were lords of the Manor of Horningsham. A large, fairly level site was chosen, and one that overlooked a large area of the parish. Shelter provided by the valley and a fresh water supply were also important. c. 1270 the Priory at Longleat was built. The land was evidently fertile, as monks always chose their sites carefully. There was fresh water nearby which supplied them with fish and they also had a rabbit warren and an orchard. The five monks lived a quiet life, but this was never a rich establishment, and by 1529 it was desolate.

Sir John Thynne bought the priory and sixty acres of land in 1540. He was cunning and ambitious and had an instinct for opportunity which enabled him to increase his wealth through accumulation. In 1548 he acquired the Manor of Horningsham and by the time of his death in 1580 the estate had grown to 6000 acres. Numerous men were employed by him and these men and their families enabled the village to grow and prosper. There are still some houses standing that were built in the 17th century.

The two main roads through the village, Water Lane leading

into Church Street and Chapel Street on to Pottle Street, developed slowly. There are hills on both sides of the latter and it is probable that the land at the bottom was farmed, the high ground was used for grazing and woodland, and the houses were built in between. The numerous lanes are further evidence of random development.

Physical development continued well into the 19th century. The population reached its peak in 1831 at 1323 and in 1861 there were 253 houses. Today there are approximately 120 houses, but although some have been demolished , in a number of cases two or three houses have been knocked into one. Since the middle of the 19th century the changes in the village have been social rather than physical. Education has encouraged people to move on to live and work elsewhere. Leisure time has increased and with it the number of social activities in the village. Families are smaller but want more space, hence the number of houses that have been joined together. Present day planning laws make further building impossible. What will the village look like in another hundred years I wonder?

Chapel St. c. 1930. In the foreground is Thorne's chair factory. Four generations of Thornes made chairs, bedsteads and brushes here from 1789-1936. There are now two semi-detatched houses on this site, built in 1947. Walter Thorne's white house is to the right. Further on is Bakery Farm and a small shop, both run by three generations of Chapmans. There is a sign on the wall advertising tea. Just visible in the top right corner is the old village hall.

The village from the road to Maiden Bradley, c. 1930. Trees dominate the landscape. Horningsham was originally developed from Selwood Forest, which is why the community is so scattered. The church, school and vicarage are all visible. To the right and behind the war memorial are the nurseries where trees were grown to be planted in the estate forests.

The Common, c. 1920. The three well trodden paths all lead to the water pump. The number of trees on the green is unusual, this area was normally an open space used for village activities. Horningsham was also fortunate enough to have a field and the old village hut nearby.

View from the Church, c. 1930. This view has changed very little. Royal Oak House, now on the extreme right, had not yet been built, and all the houses in White St. are thatched. The garden full of apple trees belongs to the manor house next to the school. In another picture I was given there were cabbages here. At this time most garden space was used for growing food. A few flowers were grown, but the seed was always kept for the next year, it was never bought.

The Foakes family outside no.9 Hollybush in 1898. In 1850 this was the Holly Tree Inn, so called because of the holly tree which remains in the garden to this day.

14 Gentle Street – 'Old Timbers' – in the snow. It may be that global warming will prevent us ever seeing icicles like this again in Wiltshire.

53 White Street. This street has always been a popular spot with photographers. Along with the village shop, I was sent more pictures of these 'chocolate box' cottages than any other. In terms of number of houses, this street has not changed in 150 years. In the 1960s the eleven houses, all built between 1600 and 1850, were sold, the new owners modernising and re-roofing them. No. 53 is the only single house. The picture above was taken c. 1942. Below is a view of the house in 1964 with its new roof. The shape of the roof and the high chimney stacks show that it was once thatched.

54/55 White Street. c. 1930. Parts of this building date back to the 17th century. The thatched semi-circular projection on the wall is a bread oven. No. 55 used to be a Dame School. Harriet Adlam ran her school from here 1870-1902. In 1878 hers was one of four Dame Schools, each with 13 pupils. She was paid 11s.11d. a year for each child. By 1902 she was only caring for children under school age, teaching them their letters. The picture below was taken in 1962, when the two cottages were bought by Mr. Powell. His wife stands outside. The present owner, Frances Chris, moved here with her parents in 1971.

Nos. 56-58 White Street., taken in 1965 from the Heaven's Gate direction. The previous view of the street in the 1930s shows the building when it was completely thatched. In 1965 the three cottages were bought by Percy and Valerie Wheeler and turned into one.

Park Farm c. 1900. For many years this 18th century farmhouse was the dairy attached to Manor Farm. The Long family farmed here from 1889-1969. The whey left over when making cheese, was piped under the road to the piggeries opposite.

66-68 Church Street. These three cottages, built c. 1700, are attached to the school. Until 1986 no. 68 was the School House, it is now the Nursery School. The cottages were built as a manor house. In 1737 it was occupied by the 2nd Viscount Weymouth, who left Longleat after the death of his young wife. He died a broken man in 1751 and is buried (at his own request) in Horningsham churchyard. No. 68 became the School House in 1844 when the school was built.

The Old Vicarage. This was pulled down in 1900 when Canon Jacob retired and was replaced by with the present building. The cottages behind were demolished c. 1875.

73-75 Church Street. These three almshouses were built during the 17th century. In 1910 the rent was 1/- a week for one room up and one down. The Misses Murch lived at no.73 from 1915 when their shop at Newbury went bankrupt. Their father Matthew kept a shop at 17 Newbury for over 30 years.

78 The Island. Holywell House was built c. 1750 by the clothier William Everett. It was later occupied by the village doctor, Dr. Bothwell.

The Round House was a wool drying house during the 18th century, to which the cottage and workshop below were originally attached. This area of the village had a large woollen mill and blanket factory, owned by the Everett family in the late 18th and early 19th centuries.

Two semi-detached cottages in Water Lane during the 1950s when they were still thatched.

90 Water Lane. Mr. and Mrs. Tom Trollope outside Rose Cottage with their family c. 1908. The children (left to right) are Ernest (later landlord of the Bath Arms), Lucy, Lizzie, Chrissie, Frances and Bill. The family lived in this cottage from 1903-1950, and Ernest later lived there with his own family. Tom's great-grandson Stephen Crossman moved there in 1986, and he in turn swopped with his parents John and Vera in 1997.

Mill Farm. The Mill ceased working in 1909. Before that the village flour was ground here and barley for pheasant food. The water wheel and machinery were dismantled and sold in 1910. Earlier there was a silk mill near here, probably owned by William Mears whose initials are on the wall of 86 Water Lane - WM1711.

The water pump on the Common. This is a good surviving example of a late 19th century water pump. It is cast iron with some decoration and the name of the manufacturers Owen and Son, engineers, London.

The Bath Arms. This 17th century building became a public house in 1732 when it was called the New Inn. It later changed to the Lord Weymouth Arms and then the Marquess of Bath's Arms. In 1850 there were four pubs in the village - the Bath Arms, the Royal Oak (15 Gentle St), the Holly Tree (9 Hollybush), and the George and Dragon (108 Anchor Barton). There was also an off-licence at 190 Chapel St.

Bath Arms. This is the public bar during Ernie Trollope's time as landlord. One can imagine the villagers frequenting this bar - no doubt many of them had their favourite seat! Notice the shove halfpenny board on the table.

122 Scotland: the Old Post Office. The village Post Office has had three locations. From c.1850 the Maxfield family ran the Post Office at 92 Water Lane. In 1894 it moved with them to no. 122. The Post Office stayed here until Charlie Barnes retired in 1971, when it moved to the village shop.

174 Chapel Street. Mrs Ellen Moody stands outside. She and her husband Matthew and later their son Albert lived here from 1908-1965, followed by Albert's daughter and son-in-law, Gladys and Fred Triggs, until 1994. Albert worked in the forestry at Longleat. Matthew was head carter at Lower Barn Farm.

Highwood Cottages. The three cottages at Highwood were Longleat's timber yard in the 18th century. The large area of garden behind is enclosed by a long row of sheds and a wall. In the picture are Annie Trollope and her sister visiting Mrs. Jarvis and her three daughters c. 1920.

203 Pottle Street. Evacuee Anita Waller is sitting on the wall. Like White St, the houses in Pottle St. are all privately owned. Several cottages are no longer standing. Some had weaving sheds, another a Dame School

The garden at 221 Highwood. This is the home of Gordon Taylor and his wife Leonie, who have lived there since 1960. Seventy years ago all the gardens in the village would have been filled with vegetables. Today, however, a 90 feet vegetable patch like this one is quite unusual.

County Cottage sits on the Wiltshire/Somerset border. This cottage, built 1803 by Sir Jeffry Wyatville for the 2nd Marquess of Bath, is a typical example of the once popular *cottage orné* style, i.e. the appearance of a rustic cottage. The residents Mr. and Mrs. Stay pose outside in 1952.

LONGLEAT FROM LAK

Longleat House, Gardens and Kitchen Gardens

Longleat House, like many other great English houses, began as a monastery. Augustinian Canons built their priory in the thirteenth century, and it survived until Henry VIII disolved the monasteries. The Crown then sold the priory in 1540 to Sir John Thynne for £53. Building began in 1547 but was destroyed by fire twenty years later. In 1568 Sir John began again, and by the time he died in 1580 the house was almost complete. Pevsner describes it as 'the first completely Elizabethan house, large, self-assured, all of a piece'.

Thirteen Thynnes have owned Longleat since, each making their own contribution to its history. The 1st Viscount Weymouth was a great friend of Bishop Ken who lived at Longleat for twenty years, and together they created the Bishop Ken library. The 1st Marquess employed Capability Brown to redesign the park (1757-62), and his son continued this, employing Humphrey Repton, who redesigned the shape of the Half Mile lake. The 4th Marquess travelled to Italy on many occasions, the Renaissance palaces he visited inspiring him to transform the east wing of the House.

It was the 5th Marquess who took the first steps on the road to the leisure industry with the opening of Cheddar Caves to the public. His son began the stately home industry when he opened Longleat in 1949, and in 1966 he introduced the first safari park outside Africa. The 6th Marquess also employed Russell Page to rearrange the gardens, and together they created Longcombe Drive, with rhododendrons and azaleas, as the principle entrance to the park.

The present Marquess planted the longest maze in the world in 1975, and two smaller ones since. He is also a writer and painter, and the walls of his apartments in the House are decorated with his own murals.

Longleat House c. 1920 when it was just a family home.The left side has since been made into a private garden surrounded by a hedge. The roads have been altered to accomodate the thousands of tourists who now visit each year.

Longleat Lodge. This was built c. 1804 by Sir Jeffrey Wyatville for the 2nd Marquess of Bath as an impressive approach to Longleat from Horningsham. The single storey extension in this picture is much later, and the one later added to the right was built in 1947.

The north garden and Orangery c. 1925. The Orangery was built c. 1805 by the architect Sir Jeffrey Wyatville to a design by the 2nd Marchioness. He also built the stables, butchery and boathouse. The main axes of the garden still preserve the original design, but bedding fashions have changed considerably. Significant changes were made before the House opened to encourage visitors to wander. More recently the 7th Marquess has created a love maze.

Heaven's Gate and the view to the House were created by Capability Brown. Bishop Thomas Ken came to live at Longleat in 1691 having been deprived of his see of Bath and Wells for refusing to take the oath of allegiance to William and Mary in 1688. He died at Longleat in 1711 and is buried at Frome.

Longleat Fire Brigade in 1881. It was important for large country houses to have their own fire engine as they were too far away from the engines in the towns. Thankfully there was never a fire at Longleat - an engine this size would not have had much effect. Kenneth Carpenter, a gardener until 1967, could only remember this being used to water the flower beds!

Above: Re-consecration of Glastonbury Abbey, 1909. The Prince and Princess of Wales were guests at this event and took the opportunity to visit Longleat. Also in the picture are the Archbishop of Canterbury and Lord and Lady Bath with four of their children. Lady Emma stands second from left, Lady Kathleen far right, Lady Bath is seated to the right of Princess Mary and Lady Mary and Lord Henry are sitting on the ground.

Left: Lord Weymouth, son of the 5th Marquess. This is a copy of the card given to each of Longleat's tenants when he was killed. Many years later Weymouth's younger brother Henry was to recall the fear and apprehension he felt at the prospect of caring for Longleat.

Lord Alexander Thynne was a younger brother of the 5th Marquess. A bachelor, he lived at Norton Hall near Northampton, and was MP for Bath. His collection of Dutch paintings and 10,000 books are now housed at Longleat.

L^T COLONEL · LORD · ALEXANDER · THYNNE D.S.O.
Born February 17th 1873

Served in the SOUTH·AFRICAN·WAR 1900-1902
In the SOMALILAND·CAMPAIGN 1903-1904
Served with the Wiltshire Yeomanry in FRANCE from 1915 to 1916

Commanded the Wiltshire Regiment from 1916 until he was killed, on September 14th 1918 near BETHUNE.

He was twice wounded — 1916 and 1918
Mentioned in Despatches

He was Secretary to the Lieut Governor of the Orange River Colony 1902-1905
He was Member for the City of Bath and the London County Council.

The family of the 5th Marquess of Bath c. 1915. Standing are Lady Mary and John, Viscount Weymouth. Seated are Lady Kathleen, Lord Henry and Lady Emma.

Horningsham Flower Show. The 5th Marquess and Marchioness are in the front row with their son Viscount Weymouth. Major Mortimer (the Agent) and Mr. Cameron (Forester) are among those behind. Does anyone know the others?

Dick Futcher, gamekeeper. Dick Futcher was a great friend of the 6th Marquess. As a boy, Lord Henry went ratting with Futcher. Later, when he was old enough to own a motorcycle, Viscount Weymouth took Futcher on visits to the coast. Dick was probably a refreshing change from the company that Viscount Weymouth was used to keeping. He was unable to read or write, talked broad Wiltshire and enjoyed his beer: but he did know about real life, and Viscount Weymouth thoroughly enjoyed his experiences with him. Connie Bull (née Dredge) recalls playing outside her house as a child when the two men went past on the motorcycle. The bike hit a stone in the road and tipped Futcher out of the sidecar. To quote Connie, 'Dick's French was very good!'

John, Viscount Weymouth, shooting, accompanied by Charles Barter.

Viscount Weymouth's 21st birthday, 1926. Although the Viscount's birthday was in January, the official celebration took place in July during Flower Show week. It took place in the park across the lake from the House and was enjoyed by hundreds of guests. Major Mortimer, the Agent, was the organiser, helped by Mr. Long (Lord Bath's secretary) and Mr. Cameron (Forester). The bridge crossing the water between the two lawns was designed by Mr. Hughes, Clerk of the Works.

Lord and Lady Bath, with Viscount Weymouth, personally greeted every one of the guests.

A Banquet was enjoyed by family and distinguished guests at 2.30pm. The villagers of Horningsham and Corsley with their families, together with all employees and their families, were given tea. There were hundreds of guests, so tea had to be served in numerous sittings.

Presentations. Mrs. Harding and Mrs. Dicks presented Viscount Weymouth with a leather bound blotter and paper case on behalf of the women of Horningsham. Mr. Cameron presented him with a gold-mounted walking stick on behalf of the Horningsham Men's Club. Major Mortimer is also in the picture. After tea there were attractions in the park, including boating, Punch and Judy, and music from a military band. One marquee had a dance floor where hundreds enjoyed an evening of dancing. The day ended with a huge fireworks display.

The 6th Marchioness and three of her children, c. 1936. Lady Caroline is on the left, Lord Christopher on his mother's knee and Alexander, Viscount Weymouth on the right. In 1953 Lady Bath and her husband were divorced. They both remarried in the same year, Daphne to Xan Fielding and Lord Bath to Virginia Tennant.

The funeral of the 5th Marquess of Bath in 1946. Following a short family service at the House, Lord Bath was cremated at Bristol and the ashes were interred in the family vault at Longbridge Deverill church. (Longleat, although part of the civil parish of Horningsham, was originally in the ecclesiastical parish of Longbridge Deverill). The girls of the Royal School for daughters of Officers - evacuated to Longleat at the outbreak of war from Bath - formed a Guard of Honour as the coffin left the House. The pall bearers were Harold Hillier and Charlie Davis (chauffeurs), Samuel Garrett (gamekeeper), Leonard Gould (head kitchen gardener), Alfred Barrett (clerk of works) and J. Hames.

Longleat laundry, c. 1937. The laundry was in a corner of the stableyard. This picture was taken on the drying green, with the washing lines in the background. Billy Rowe, a gardener, poses with Mary Blackmore. The lady on the right is possibly Olive Pitcher. There were four laundrymaids, each having specific tasks. Two days each week were spent scrubbing the laundry - the building was on three floors and all the floors, tables, chairs and stairs were scrubbed wood. The rest of the week was spent washing and ironing. The fourth maid washed towels, sheets and tea-towels. Promotion meant you helped with the family washing. The head maid was responsible for Lord Bath's personal washing, and also the three staff under her.

Arranging flowers in the Great Hall and State Drawing Room c. 1950. Mrs. Colston Hale was a professional florist from Warminster, her trade card stating '50 years experience of successful exhibiting and judging'. Mike Carpenter worked in the kitchen gardens and was responsible for growing and delivering all the flowers for the House.

Longleat guides c. 1969. When the House first opened, members of the family acted as guides, but this soon became impracticable. Pictured left to right are Les and Doris Wheeler, Malcolm Weller, Patrick Feeney, Roger Stocks and Jack Vaughan.

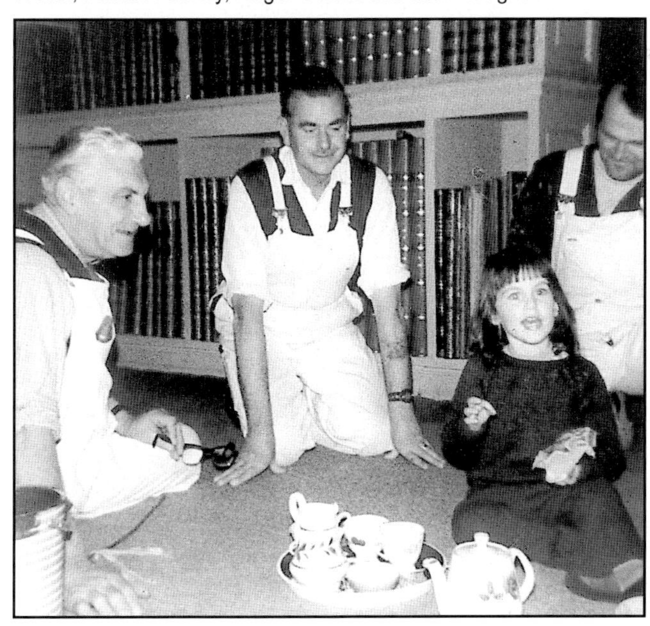

Taking tea with Lenka, c. 1973. Estate painters Bill Webb, Jim Ford and Ian McClurg enjoying afternoon tea with Lady Lenka Thynn.

Paddy Dalton and Graham Eggleton in the Secret Garden c. 1985. Paddy was Head Gardener 1974-1992. Between them is a statue of 'Sir' Jeffrey Hudson. He was court dwarf to Charles I's queen, and was presented in a pie to the king.

The 6th Marquess' 80th birthday in 1985. Head Gardener Paddy Dalton presents Lord Bath with a hornbeam which was later planted in the Pleasure Walk.

Three kitchen gardeners cease their hoeing to pose for the camera, c. 1935. Left to right are Derrick Robins, Peter Daniels and Kenneth Carpenter.

Five kitchen gardeners. Cyril Seymour, Mike Carpenter, Frank Barnes (Foreman), Wilf Found and Stan Carpenter.

The vinery. This was built c. 1870 for William Taylor, head gardener and famous viniculturalist. At 216 feet long and 18 feet high it must have been a magnificent sight when filled with ripe grapes. Unfortunately most of the glass was destroyed in the gales of 1990.

A full range of fruit, including grapes, peaches and figs, were grown. The metal labels, such as this one, are still visible on the outside walls 70 years after planting.

Crops of chrysanthemums and cabbages. The kitchen gardens cover eleven acres, at the turn of the twentieth century approximately 25 men were employed there. The gardens produced fruit, vegetables and cut flowers for the house, and bedding plants for the formal gardens and terrace pots.

In 1960 Clifford Gould took over the kitchen gardens and employed Frank Barnes, Ernest Robertson and Maurice Robertson. This picture was taken c. 1965, the staff then were Ernest, Dick Carrier, Maurice and Robert Penny.

John Abrams, HTV's gardening expert, visited Longleat in 1979. Left to right are Derek Longuet (Garden Centre manager), Paddy Dalton (Head Gardener), Maurice Robertson (grower), and John Abrams.

Clive Eggleton and Maurice Robertson in the vinery, full of fuchsias in pots instead of grapes. Longleat ran a series of annual 'Fuchsia Festivals' in the 1980s. Maurice spent all his working life in the kitchen gardens. By 1960 Lord Bath could no longer run them at a profit, and so leased the gardens to Clifford Gould. In 1970 Clive joined Maurice and his wife Evelyn, growing fuchsias, tomatoes, cucumbers and other plants to sell in Mr. Gould's garden centre at Longleat. When the gardens and centre reverted to Longleat in 1975, Maurice and Clive stayed on until 1988 when Maurice finished and Clive moved to the flower gardens. The kitchen garden greenhouses were filled with fuchsias, including the four varieties Anna of Longleat, Lenka of Longleat, Scion of Longleat and Frome in Bloom, all bred by Maurice.

Church and Chapel

To stand on the steps outside the west door of this church is to understand what someone meant who once remarked, 'This church looks lovingly upon her people'. To the right are the pretty cottages in White Street, and straight ahead a clear view of Longleat Park and the House. Apart from the removal of some trees, the scene in this picture has changed very little in seventy years.

The parish church of St. John the Baptist has stood here since 1154. Of the original building, only those parts of the fifteenth century tower that have not undergone restoration remain. It was extensively rebuilt in 1844, the cost being met by Harriet, Marchioness of Bath.

The main reason for rebuilding was that the previous church was not considered big enough. The church census taken in 1851 records 302 people attending Morning Service. In 1910 services were still well attended, by the Family from Longleat House, servants, tenant farmers and other villagers. Lord Bath read the lesson and the singing was led by a choir of ten men and ten boys. The organist and choir master then was schoolmaster Thomas Welborn. The congregation was welcomed into the church by a peal of bells.

The picture today is very different - no choir, no bells, and an average congregation of ten. However, as a Christian community we remain positive and look forward. The church is still open for worship every Sunday and each Wednesday there is a service of Evening Prayer. Once a month we have an informal Village Service which attracts upwards of sixty people.

Throughout its long life Horningsham Church has always received generous financial support from the Thynne family, and there has always been a small group of villagers dedicated to running the church. We hope this commitment continues for many years to come.

Above: **Two girls in their Sunday best** pose for the photographer in the churchyard c. 1900. Although only sixty years since its restoration, ivy already covers part of the church walls. A tomb on the left of the picture has iron railings; these were all removed during the Second World War.

Left: **Church interior c. 1930**. This view from the gallery at the west end successfully captures a sense of light and space. The oak pews shine in the sunlight, reflecting one hundred years of vigorous polishing. Electric light was not installed until 1938, so oil lamps were still in use. The Lady Chapel was created during the 1960s to make an area for the Sunday School. This picture shows the original pews in this area facing north.

Rev. Francis Skurray, vicar 1797-1848. He was extremely popular with the villagers and worked hard to look after both their spiritual and physical needs. He was keen to improve the appearance of the church, paying the clerk extra to clean it and also a man to cut the churchyard grass. Skurray enjoyed walking the countryside and he published a book of sermons and a book of poems.

Canon James Jacob, vicar 1858-1900. He continued the work of improving the church, being responsible for tiling the floor, installing new light fittings, having the lych gate built and enlarging the churchyard. Jacob retired to Salisbury in 1900 and died there in 1909. Like Skurray, his death prompted generous tributes in the local press, emphasizing how popular he had been with both his parishioners and his fellow clergy. The stained glass window at the west end of the church was erected in his memory in 1911.

Rev. Arthur Murray, vicar 1900-1930. He was to be the last vicar to occupy the living for a period in excess of ten years. One of his major achievements was a new heating system, installed in 1928. There is a plaque to his memory in the Chancel. Murray died in 1932, and is buried next to Francis Skurray at the south east corner of the church.

Mr. and Mrs. Kenneth Carpenter. Mr. Carpenter was born in Horningsham in 1897. He spent most of his working life in Longleat's kitchen gardens, finally retiring from the flower gardens in 1967. He took up the post of Sexton in 1943, and his wife Florence was the cleaner. In 1965, when she gave up this work, her husband took over. He continued as Sacristan and cleaner until 1977, when ill health forced him to retire. Mr. Carpenter died in 1981. The post died with him.

Canon Anthony Johnson, vicar 1976-1985. The last vicar to live in Horningsham and have sole care of the parish was Claude Foster-Palmer, who left in 1955. We then joined with Maiden Bradley until 1976, when Rev. John Wright retired and Horningsham was joined with Warminster. Canon Johnson was appointed vicar of the Minster, Warminster and Upton Scudamore in 1967. He moved to Semley in 1985 and retired to Tisbury in 1992.

Canon Roger Sharpe, vicar 1986-2000. Canon Sharpe saw the size of his parish increase greatly during his fourteen years in office. In 1992 his original three parishes increased to five with the inclusion of Corsley and Chapmanslade. In 1995 the Cley Hill Team was created when the vicar of the Deverills, the Rev. Nicholas von Benzon, became Team Vicar. The Team then consisted of ten churches. In 2000 Canon Sharpe and his wife Mary retired to East Grimstead near Salisbury.

Rev. Alison Wadsworth. Rev. Wadsworth spent her working life as a teacher, and was Headmistress of Horningsham School 1986-1996. She was ordained Deacon in 1997 and Priested in 1998. Although living in Warminster and based at the Minster, Alison holds a great affection for Horningsham and very involved in the life of the parish.

Rev. Richard Yates. Richard Yates moved to Horningsham in 1962 when he started his work as a dentist at The Chantry in Warminster, retiring in 1991. Richard was ordained Deacon in 1999, and devoted himself to the care of Horningsham. His ordination at Salisbury Cathedral was a very moving occasion, and Horningsham felt justifiably proud of its first 'home grown' priest.

The precise date of the building of the Chapel has always been a subject for discussion, as unfortunately no records survive before 1700. The traditional view is that it was built in 1566 by a group of Scottish Presbyterian stonemasons who were working for Sir John Thynne on the building of Longleat House. When Sir John learned that the men held their prayer meetings in a nearby wood, he allowed them to build the Chapel.

Those who doubt the authenticity of this argue that Sir John had no need to send to Scotland when there were good builders in the Cotswolds. But perhaps the Scots came of their own accord, or may have been working on such buildings as Lacock Abbey, as John Chapman was when invited to assist at Longleat. The names of the workmen recorded in the Longleat account books show that many families, Trollope, Marsh, Thorne, Ford, Carpenter, Adlam and Chapman for example, have been involved in the life of the Chapel for four hundred years.

The Chapel has been extended and renovated numerous times. In 1754 it was enlarged at the east end, and in 1816 at the west end. In 1863 the work comprised a new floor, new pews, thatching and general decoration. The congregation raised some of the money, but most came from generous individuals and sister churches. Thatching and re-flooring took place again in 1935, and in 1959 the roof was repaired and thatched with Norfolk reed. The Chapel was last thatched in 1989.

Like the Church, the Chapel's congregations have got smaller. The last full-time minister left in 1969, since when visiting ministers have preached each Sunday. On a daily basis the Chapel is cared for by Barbara Carpenter, who has worshipped there all her life. It is a fact that the Chapel is the oldest free church in England still open for worship. Long may it continue.

Thatching c. 1950. One of the conditions of the Chapel lease is that it must be regularly thatched. For many years this highly skilled work was done by George Beauchamp (on the roof) and his brother-in-law Albert Moody (on the ladder). Some six tons of straw were needed and over 7000 spars. The Beauchamps lived at 190 Chapel St for over seventy years. John Dicks previously ran a grocery business and off licence there; when he died in 1889 George's parents took the business over. Charles Beauchamp was a thatcher by trade, but also ran a small farm, shop and the off licence known as The Crescent. After Charles's death his wife Annie ran the off licence, and son George farmed and thatched. His brother Thomas lived at Mill Farm. Over the years, George and Tom between them were described in Kelly's trade directory as carpenter, blacksmith, coal merchant, farmer, undertaker, thatcher and beer retailer.

Annual grass cutting, June 1951. Until 1965 the grass in this graveyard and in the one across the road from the Chapel was cut once a year by the men of the village using scythes and reaphooks. Pictured left to right are Roy Trollope, Ken Doel, Sid Carpenter, Stan Davis, Tom Trollope, Percy Edwards, George Beauchamp, Rev. Albert Banton, Stan Ford, Bill Cox, Fred Chapman, Billy Rowe, Derrick Robins, Reg Rideout, Albert Moody, Walt Clark and Alfie Marsh.

The Chapel was most recently thatched in 1989. Five men are working on the roof, while their families sit and watch. £50,000 was spent over the following two years on thatching, releading windows, drainage and decoration.

Decorated for Harvest Festival c.1930. The pulpit is beautifully decorated with the village's finest flowers and vegetables. Also in the picture is a small hand-blown organ bought in 1920.

Harvest Festival c.1982. The emphasis here is on flowers, reflecting the fact that fewer people grew their own vegetables. A traditional harvest loaf stands at the front of the display.

Mr. and Mrs. Thomas Trollope. Mr. Trollope, who died in 1934, was a deacon and Sunday school superintendent for thirty three years. He spent his working life in the flower gardens at Longleat and also arranged the flowers in the House. His son Ernie ran the Bath Arms for many years, and granddaughter Vera married John Crossman, a local farmer. This picture shows Mr. and Mrs. Trollope dressed in their Sunday best, seated at a table in the Chapel.

Chapel Womens Guild 1956. This was founded in 1937. It folded c.1970, following the death in 1969 of Mabel Chapman, a founder member and secretary for thirty years. Pictured from the back, left to right, are Mabel Chapman, Violet Marsh, Catherine Dicks, Lily Beauchamp, Mrs. Goring, Mrs. Mathews, Mrs. Barratt, Mrs. Ford, Mrs. Brown, Annie Stevens, Margaret Barratt, Lily Ford, Barbara Carpenter, Mary Russell, Margaret Summerell, Joan Dix and Mrs. Carpenter.

A new organ was bought in 1958, and dedicated at the Good Friday Gathering on 4th April. Pictured are Mr. Aplin who assembled the organ, Catherine Dicks, Rev. Archie Kew (Chapel Minister) and Rev. Basil Sims (Bristol).

Barbara Carpenter plays the organ at the annual reunion in 1999. She has been the Chapel organist since c1955.

The 1999 reunion service in the Chapel. Among those pictured are the Rev. Richard Yates, Monica Foreman, Margaret Long, Carol Cox (née Robins), Joe and Beryl Lovatt, Dolly Ferry, Mr and Mrs Martin Pring, Mr and Mrs Will Found and their daughter Diane Baldwin and niece Kathleen Pickup (née Alford) and Pam Body (née Cobbold).

Also at the reunion pictured from the front are Leonie Taylor, Ernest Chapman and his daughter, Mr. and Mrs. David Carpenter, Mr. and Mrs. Harold Howlett, Mr. and Mrs. Irvin Edwards, Mrs. Cheeseman (granddaughter of Tom Trollope) and her family, Mr. and Mrs. Albert Honey, Caroline Stroud (née Trollope), Lesley Trollope, Jane Yates, Tim Moore, Michael Trollope and John Crossman.

HORNINGSHAM SCHOOL.

School

The Factory Act of 1844 not only prohibited the employment of children under eight in textile factories, but also laid down that children between the ages of eight and thirteen who worked in the factories must attend an approved elementary school for three hours a day. The following year Lord Bath's School was opened and financed by him. In 1858 it was visited by Her Majesty's Inspectors. There were just 40 children, taught by a master and a mistress in one room with a flagged floor.

In 1870 the Elementary Education Act was passed, giving every child of school age a school place in a building of reasonable quality, with a qualified head teacher. The existing voluntary school bodies were given six months to make good any shortfall in these requirements in their own schools and only if such gaps were not made good would the new 'board' schools be set up. To avoid any inter-denominational squabbles, board schools were to be non-sectarian. The school boards were also empowered to introduce school attendance by-laws covering children aged five to twelve, but these were not compulsory.

School fees still had to be paid - usually 1d or 2d a week - and this was strongly resented, some parents simply keeping their children at home in order to avoid paying; in Horningsham some parents chose to continue sending their children to one or other of the four dame schools in the village.

A further Act of 1876 was intended to make school attendance genuinely compulsory, at least up to the age of ten, but even then the necessary by-laws were sometimes not passed in certain areas and it was not until the 1880 Education Act that school attendance was finally made compulsory for every child of school age. The minimum leaving age was raised to eleven in 1893 and to twelve in 1899. Not until 1918 was the leaving age raised to fourteen.

By 1892 most children were attending the National Church of England School and it was enlarged to take 200 pupils. In 1907, by which time education was free, there were 140 pupils. When the inspectors visited the school in 1921 Mr. Welborn was headmaster. They found him to be a pleasant man and a good musician, but he was not a good teacher and discipline was poor. The situation improved with the arrival of Mr. Sutton in 1921 and Miss Anderson a year later, but the former only stayed until 1928.

The twenties were a period of change for the school. There were four different head teachers and in 1926 the school was taken over by Wiltshire County Council. Both Mrs. Hersee and Miss Anderson found it difficult to cope with the older children. The school became a junior department in 1931, and so Miss Anderson was happy to remain headmistress. The arrival of Mrs. Holly in 1937 was the beginning of 28 years of stability and happiness.

Both these ladies retired in 1965 and were replaced by Alan Booker and his wife Monica. On the occasion of their retirement Mr. Booker was to remark how fond of his wife all the children were, sometimes calling her Mum. Life was very different when you moved into the junior class. Pupils recall that the headmaster was pleasant and had a good sense of humour, but he was also respected and feared. School was happy and enjoyable for those who worked hard and behaved themselves, but there was trouble if you didn't!

In 1973 school life changed again with the arrival of Tim Hill. He was only 27, with a young family, and took a much more relaxed approach to the job. I cannot recall anyone being smacked. Changes in the curriculum included scientific experiments, a story at the end of each day, swimming lessons, school trips and walking around the village to discover our past.

Mr. Hill left the school in 1982. John Roseamon came for two terms, followed by Paul Buckley for three years. 1986 saw the arrival of Alison Wadsworth, who felt it was important to build strong links with other rural schools and also with the church.

She was responsible for broadening the curriculum, which increased pupil numbers.

The present headmistress, Sue Ivey, arrived in 1996. Under her leadership the school is flourishing. She has seen the new classroom built for the reception class, so that the school runs on three classes, with a school roll in June 2000 of 67 children. Her energy and enthusiasm are reflected in the attitude of the children, who continue to be a credit to the school.

Annual School Treat 1897. In July the children from the church day school and Sunday school were given their annual treat. After a short service in the church at 3.00pm everyone enjoyed tea on the vicarage lawn. They then went to a nearby field where swings and other amusements were provided. The boys played cricket, and then played a match left-handed against the girls. The latter won easily, due to excellent bowling by Miss Welborn. The games lasted until 8.00pm, when the school bell was rung to tell the children it was time to go home. Canon Jacob is seated in the front with a child on his knee. Thomas Welborn the schoolmaster is to his right.

A class in 1901. The date on the blackboard is 25th November 1901.

School in 1904. Some of the children pose for the photographer after school.

School girls c. 1905. This is quite an unusual picture, as the children are normally grouped in classes. I presume that somewhere is a picture of all the boys!

The middle class in 1911. The school was divided into three classes: infants, standards I-III (7-10 year olds) and standards IV-VII (11-14 year olds).

'Eat more vegetables' 1928. An infant welfare exhibition was held in Warminster at the Town Hall. This picture is from a play performed to encourage children to eat more vegetables. The 'onion' standing second from the right is Sybil Baverstock, later Mrs. Alec Long.

Everyone remembers Miss Anderson with affection and respect. She came to the school in 1922, having previously cycled 20 miles from Barford St Martin with her brother to enquire about the job. At this time there were three classes aged 5-14. Mr. Sutton was the headmaster and taught the older children, while Miss Anderson taught the middle class. He left in 1928 and was replaced by Mrs. Hersee who stayed for just two years. Miss Anderson became headmistress in 1930. The following year Horningsham became a junior department and children over eleven completed their education at The Avenue School in Warminster. This suited Miss Anderson; the school inspector had reported that she found the older children difficult to cope with. They in turn no doubt found it difficult to cope with the discipline imposed by Mr. Dewey at Warminster!

The following photographs were all taken during the 1920s. They are all named from the back row to the front, and from left to right.

c. 1926. Mr. Sutton, ?, ?, ?, Eddie Ball, Ronald Barter, Sidney Batson, Stan Doel and Miss Anderson. Evelyn Carpenter, Grace Carrier, Stella Doel, Phyllis King, Sissy Garrett, Eadie Howlett, ? and Vera Foakes. Charlie Carpenter, ?, Laura Carpenter, Margaret Long, Harold Marsh and Roy Trollope.

c. 1926. Mr. Sutton, Cecil Alford, Mike Carpenter, Ernest Allard, Derrick Robins, Freddie Weeks, Ivor Ball and Miss Anderson. Sydney Carpenter, Arthur Ford, Jack Timms, Dorothy Doel, Dora Curtis, Phyllis Watts, Denis Froud and Francis Ford. Dorothy Price, Rose King, Hilda Carpenter, Margaret Robins and Ena Carpenter.

c. 1927. Leslie Garrett, ?, ?, George Mathews, Denis Gooding, Douglas Dicks and Miss Anderson. Margery Marsh, Joan King, Sybil Carpenter, Doris Cox, Kathleen Trollope, Jean Watts, Kathleen Batson, Madge Watts and Reg King. Arthur Carpenter, ?, Betty Chapman, Ruby Carrier, ?, Dorothy Carpenter and ?.

c. 1927. Arthur Ford, Ivor Ball, Mike Carpenter, Cecil Alford, Jack Timms and Francis Ford. Ronald Barter, Phyllis King, Sissy Garrett, Margaret Robins, Rose King, Dora Curtis, Dorothy Doel, Dorothy Price, ?, Stella Doel, Eadie Howlett and ?. ?, ?, Margaret Long, ?, Evelyn Carpenter and Vera Foakes. Charlie Carpenter, Eddie Ball, ?, Sidney Batson, Harold Marsh and Sidney Carpenter.

c. 1928. Denis Gooding, Charlie Carpenter, Tom Price, Eddie Ball, Arthur Ford, George Mathews, ? and Miss Anderson. Doris Cox, Sybil Carpenter, Mildred Hillier, Stella Doel, Grace Carrier, Hilda Carpenter, Vera Foakes, Margery Marsh and ?. Jean Watts, Betty Chapman, Joan King, Kathleen Trollope, Evelyn Carpenter and Dorothy Carpenter.

c. 1929. Ted Trollope, ?, Ken Doel, Tom Price, George Mathews, Eric Mathews and Miss Anderson. Vera Bailey, Kathleen Batson, Betty Chapman, Mollie Head, Millie Hillier, Kathleen Trollope, Jean Watts and Dorothy Carpenter. Kathleen Gooding, Joyce Chapman, Catherine Beauchamp, Marion Gooding, Ruby Carrier and Madge Watts. Wilf Found, Reg King, Arthur Carpenter, Leslie Garrett and Sidney Batson.

c. 1928. Miss Windo taught the infants from 1928- 1935. Ron Cox, ?, Ken Doel, ?, Jim Ford, Denis Gooding and Miss Windo. Ted Trollope, Reg King, ?, Les Garrett, Violet Price and Wilf Found. Betty Carpenter, ?, James Carpenter, Catherine Beauchamp, Ruth Gooding and Joyce Chapman.

c. 1930. This was the last year children over eleven were at the school. ?, Bill Bailey, Harold Doman, Jack Whatley, Ken Doel, Eric Mathews, Ted Trollope, ? and Miss Anderson. Dulcie Crooms, Violet Price, Catherine Beauchamp, Violet Mullins, Joyce Chapman, Kathleen Gooding, Joan Doman and Peggy Crooms. Kathleen Batson, Olive Trollope, Betty Carpenter, Ruth Gooding and Phyllis Doman. Arthur Carpenter, Denis Gooding, Ernest Chapman, Ron Ford and ?.

c. 1929. Cliff Carpenter, Ron Ford, David Carpenter, Ron Cox, Jack Whatley, Ray Garrett and Miss Windo. Olive Trollope, Ruth Gooding, ?, ?, Sylvia Trollope and Mollie Carpenter. Harold Howlett, ?, ? and Bernard Penny.

c. 1933. Emily Doman, Dulcie Croom, Joan Doman, Mollie Carpenter, Joyce Chapman, Jean Phelps, Phyllis Doman, Sylvia Trollope and Peggy Croom. Vera Mullins, Ron Ford, David Carpenter, Ron Cox, Peter Croom, Eric Mathews, Frank Ford, Jack Whatley, Bill Hebditch and Violet Price. John Gooding, Betty Carpenter, Phyllis Carpenter, Ruth Gooding, Muriel Gould and Ernest Chapman. Harold Howlett, Bernard Penny, Cliff Carpenter and Cyril Dicks.

c. 1934. Miss Windo, Barbara Moody, Jean Edwards, Helen Davis, Eileen Carpenter, Margaret Garrett and Mary Carpenter. Roy Trollope, Lionel Marsh, ? Hebditch, Leslie Garrett, Bill Bailey, Maurice Robertson, Billy Baggs and Gordon Carpenter. Donald Hill, Stanley Carpenter, Hazel Carpenter, Victor Marsh and Tom Baggs. ? Hebditch and Irvin Edwards.

c. 1939. Eileen Cruse, Marion Hill, Eileen Carpenter, Helen Davis, Margaret Garrett, Jill Peet, Hazel Carpenter and Beryl Doman. Alfred Berry, Michael Baggs, Irvin Edwards, Donald Hill, Stanley Carpenter, Lionel Marsh, David Kemp, Denis Howlett, Donald Marsh, Billy Baggs, Jim Crees, Victor Trollope and Gordon Carpenter. Pamela Hill, Cyril Hinks, Janet Carpenter, Kathleen Barnes, Leslie Hinks, Barbara Wright, Vera Trollope and Alan Baggs. Alan Marsh, Norman Edwards, Victor Marsh, Tom Baggs, Philip Marsh, Albert Collins, John Garrett and Philip Peet.

c. 1948. Margaret Larder, Sylvia Larder, Margaret Long, Angela Tant, Anne Carpenter, Barbara Heasman, Teresa Jones, Nicola Pring, Valerie Taylor, June Long, ?, June Roberts, Valerie Churchill and Joy Churchill. Tommy Eggleton, David Taylor, Norman Price, Martin Pring, David Snelgrove, Maurice Pitman, Ray Edwards and Robert Ford.

c. 1948. Esther Rowe, Joan Dix, Glynis Evans, Marion Rideout, Janet Dredge, Margaret Eggleton and Kathleen Alford. Edward Carpenter, Malcolm Jones, Michael Trollope, Tony Adlam, Brian Carpenter, Keith Davis, Graham Long and David Pritchard.

c. 1935. This picture is part of Miss Anderson's collection, but she could not remember the event. It may be celebrating George V's silver jubilee, as one child is holding a flag. Miss Anderson did remember the school buying a new flag. Does anyone recall this?

A visit to Mill Farm c. 1964. Some of the children went to the farm to see the new born lambs. (l-r) Pauline Mathews, Faith Larkin, Lynn Carpenter, Cynthia Trollope, Margaret Ashley, Glenda Marsh, Gillian Horder, Doreen Mathews, Thelma Hardiman and Alison Dix.

c. 1965. This was Miss Anderson and Mrs. Holly's last year together. The lady on the far right is Miss Smith, a classroom helper who was to remain at the school until c. 1980. Among the pupils in this picture are Clive Eggleton, Alistair Garrett, Glenda Marsh, Andrew Bowen, Gillian Horder, Stephen and Peter Crossman, Marina Rood, Neil Carpenter, Faith Larkin, Gordon Yarde, David Clark, Alison Dix, Margaret Ashley, Thelma Hardiman, Ian Yarde, Kevin Marsh, Chris Snook, Tim Berry and John Baggs.

Miss Anderson's retirement. This television set was her retirement gift.

Introduction of school uniform. Mrs. Booker came to the school as infant teacher in September 1965 when Mrs. Holly retired. She spent one term with Miss Anderson, who retired at Christmas, while Mr. Booker took over as headmaster in January 1966. He immediately introduced the first school uniform, using the Thynne family colours of black and gold, with the family crest as the blazer badge. Amongst those in this 1966 picture are Susan and Tina Hoddinott, Martin Ashley, Stephen and Peter Crossman, Alistair Garrett, Neil Roseweir, Andrew Riley, Nick Jones, Bridget Ashley, Gerald Marsh, Kim Bond, Russell Wheeler, Andrew Bowen, Chris Snook, Dennis Marsh, Kevin Marsh, Faith Larkin, Cynthia Trollope and Pauline Tiffin.

Leavers Outing. In July 1966 Mr. Booker took his first Horningsham leavers on an outing to Cheddar. Pictured left to right are Mr. Booker, Neil Carpenter, Gordon Yarde, Clive Eggleton, David Clark, Glenda Marsh, Thelma Hardiman and (sat in front) Alison Dix and Margaret Ashley.

Leavers Outing. In July 1971 the children were taken to the QE2. They are Mr. Booker, Dennis Marsh, Richard Young, Bridget Ashley, Katrina Weeks, Ian Yarde, Mrs. Bignall and Peter Clark in front.

A game of rounders, c. 1972. This was a favourite game at playtime in the summer with the girls and the infants. (The older boys played football and cricket on their own half of the playground). Among those cheering the runners are Enver Mehmet, Trudi Hardiman, Suzanne Young, Linda Allard, Sarah Green, Helen Taylor, Caroline Stansbie, Jackie Crossman and Dale Pollard.

The school in 1972. This was Mr. and Mrs. Booker's last year. It was also the last year that the eleven plus exam was in operation. Those who passed went to Frome Grammar, the rest to Kingdown Secondary Modern. From the back, left to right, are Enver Mehmet, Susan Trollope, Teresa Ashley, Joanne Summerell, Alexander Mackintosh, David Yates, Linda Allard, Sarah Green, Catherine Bignall, Mark Young, Charlie Yates, Andrew Trollope, Paul Saxbee, Hassan Mehmet, Trudi Hardiman, Kenton Baker, Debbie Bond, Helen Taylor, Richard Ashley, Martin Weeks, Philip Ashley, Mark Horder, Lester Carpenter, Mark Haskell, Kim Bond, David Green, Stephen Baker, Robert Mackintosh, Dominic Charles, Martin Ashley, Sharon Dalton, Jacqueline Crossman, Wendy Mathews, Suzanne Young, Julie McHardy, Mrs. Bignall, Mr. and Mrs. Booker, Sarah Chard, Susan Eggleton, Caroline Stansbie, Tina Hoddinott, Della Weeks, Lucy Green, Stephen Davies, Ben Haskell, Tracey Pollard and Dale Pollard.

The school in 1975. When Mr. Hill arrived he held a meeting to outline to parents his plans for the school. One of the decisions made was that a uniform was not necessary, so after just seven years the children went back to wearing clothes of their choice. Pictured from the back are Miss Heath, Ben Haskell, Enver Mehmet, Andrew Trollope, Shaun Williams, Hassan Mehmet, Martin Weeks, Stephen Davies, Dale Pollard, Mark Young, Miss Smith, Dawn Pollard, Amanda Garton, Della Weeks, Lucy Green, Joanne Summerell, Helen Taylor, Linda Allard, Mr. Hill, Susan Trollope, Sarah Green, Teresa Ashley, Karen Abel, Tracey Pollard, Sarah Williams, Frances Batley, ?, Martin Young, ?, Lenka Thynn, Sharon Bond, Sarah Davies, Stephanie Long, ?, Charlotte ?, Sara Marfleet, Nick Hill, ?.

Cycling proficiency in 1982. Mr. Hill introduced extra curricular activities to the school. The children kept rabbits, went for local history walks around the village and had swimming lessons in Warminster. They also took their cycling proficiency test. At first all cycling lessons were in the playground, but in later years pupils took to the roads as well. The 6th Marquess of Bath presents certificates to (left to right) Michael Hall, Matthew Palma, Jeremy Trollope, James Hearley, Elizabeth White, Jim Hill, Helen Bond, Stephen Noall, Mark Strong, William Mackintosh, Paul Penny, Sarah Hearley and Nicola Gillingham.

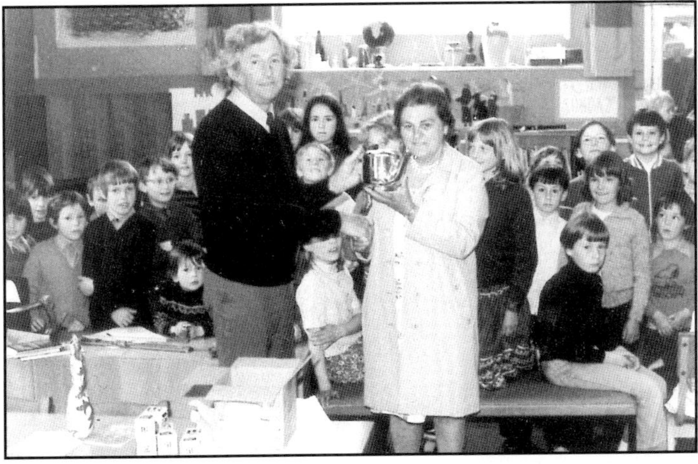

Mrs. Roberts' retirement. Georgina Roberts first went to the school as a six year old pupil in 1920. She looked after the children at lunchtime for 19 years. Mrs. Roberts retired in June 1979 and was presented with a Picquot Ware teapot and a pound of tea by John Crossman, Chairman of the School Governors.

Mrs. Ford's retirement. Mary Ford became the school cleaner in 1950 after Miss Anderson had met her in the village one day and persuaded her to do it. She retired at Christmas in 1981 and was presented with a clock radio. It was estimated that in 30 years Mrs. Ford had used 606 dusters and 1,112 tins of polish. She had also seen the number of pupils halved, from 70 to 35.

Mr. Hill's last day. Mr. Hill left at Easter in 1982, but he and his wife still live in the village. He was presented with a Georgian tea tray and a brass door knocker.

The school in 1983. Mr. Hill was followed by Mr. Roseamon. He stayed for two terms and was replaced by Paul Buckley. Pictured are Helen Hunt, Angela Saxbee, ?, Clovis Patten, Stephen Noall, Sarah Hearley, Maxine Strong, Michael Hall, Matthew Palma, Paul Penny, Jeremy Trollope, Ben Windel, Nicola Gillingham and Paul Buckley. (Middle row) Ceawlin Thynn, Philip Noall, Dominic Patten, Helen Bond, ?, Nicola Penny, Dawn Pearce, Simon Palma, Matthew Trollope, Gareth Davies, Philip Long and William Mackintosh. (Front row) Sam Patten, Mark Eggleton, Andrew Hearley, Tom Windel, Sam Hill, Nicholas Young, Karen Penny, Oliver Radford, Charlotte Ridley, ?, Lee Strong, Simon Eggleton, Nathan Noall, Shane Dix, ?, ?.

Mrs. Wadsworth's first day. The children surround their new headmistress on the first day of term in 1986. Her predecessor had introduced a navy blue sweatshirt for the children to wear, and this was a basis for the new uniform. Pictured are Tom Windel, Simon Palma, Sam Courtney, Andrew Hearley, Stuart Dix, Steven Ridley, Matthew Trollope, Mark Eggleton, Gareth Davies and Kathleen Bligdon. (Front) Alison Wadsworth, Maxine Strong, ?, Dawn Pearce and Nicola Penny.

School in 1986. At this time there were still fewer than 40 children on the roll. (Back row) Philip Long, Matthew Trollope, Andrew Hearley, Maxine Strong, Ben Windel, Dawn Pearce, Mark Eggleton, Sam Courtney, Gareth Davies and Simon Palma. (Second row) Simon Eggleton, Sam Hill, Tom Windel, Nicola Penny, Steven Rigby, Kathleen Bligdon, Stuart Dix, Sam Patten and Philip Noall. (Third row) Frances Young, Eleanor Courtney, Michael Bligdon, Stephanie Rigby, Suzanne Carver, Alison Wadsworth, Paula Ridley, Wayne Dix, Helen Bayliss and Charlotte Ridley. (Front row) Karen Penny, Shaun Bligdon, Nicholas Young, Lee Ridley, Claire Bates and Shane Dix.

Sports Day 1986. The annual school sports day is an important event in the school year. Everyone hopes for sunshine and the children look forward to an afternoon free of lessons. The school has a field next to it, and this has been marked with a running track. The sports chosen are traditional, and here the skipping race is in full flow.

School leavers on the steps of Longleat House in 1986. The children still benefit from a charity set up in 1698 by Jeremiah Crey to teach poor children to read and write. The income from a piece of land in Kingston Deverill helps to fund major school projects and also buys each school leaver a book. It used to be a dictionary, but now the children visit the bookshop and choose their own. They go to Longleat to receive their book, which is signed and presented to them by Lord Bath. (Back row) Nicola Penny, Maxine Strong, Dawn Pearce. (Middle) Matthew Trollope, Simon Palma, Ben Windel. (Front) Gareth Davies and Philip Long.

The infant classroom in 1987. There is a lovely selection of books and artwork decorates the wall. The sand tray is in the same position as it was twenty years earlier! Kirsty Yeo sharpens her pencil.

Sports teams in 1992. Competing in sport is an important part of education, but the village schools are often unable to raise a full football or netball team. Mrs. Wadsworth decided to join with other rural schools to form small teams of both sexes that could play each other. This meant any child could play either sport and represent their school at a competitive level. They played in a red and white strip because another school was already wearing blue. The netball team with Janet Hayward are Eleanor Courtney, Karen Bensley, Kim Benham, Louise Woodland, Athlene Earle, Natasha Evans and Victoria Crossman.

Pond dipping in 1992. Carole Hill helped the children to make their own garden within the school house garden beyond the playground. Pond dipping with Carole are Matthew Dixon, Christina Earle and Andrew Evans.

Barnardo's competition 1993. The charity organised a sponsored grow of runner beans. Viscount Weymouth, a past pupil of the school, was invited to measure the beans, along with Sally Hendry from Barnardos. Mark Dixon was the winner with a bean measuring 2.5m. Simon Bates and Oliver Moore were the runners up.

The school in 1993. (Back row) Amy Crossman, Natasha Evans, Simon Bates, Matthew Trollope, Rhys Lewis, Alexander Moore, Vicky Crossman, Alex Strong, James Williams and Mark Dixon. (Second row) Michelle Turney, Vicky Smith, Paul Hines, Limara Ball, Matthew Dixon, Christina Earle, Edward Earle, Karl Widdows and Rose Thomas. (Third row) Louisa Daniels, Poppy Seymour, Laura-Jane Smith, Kirsty Yeo, Jane Williams, Alison Wadsworth, Janet Hayward, Beth Thomas, Scarlett Garton, Kirsty Smith and Fiona Eggleton. (Front row) Oliver Moore, David Crossman, Andrew Evans, Leon Widdows, Philip Allard and Matthew Crossman.

Opening of the School House Nursery. The Nursery School opened in 1993. The ceremony took place in September, and the ribbon was cut by Lady Lenka Thynn. After short speeches by Lady Lenka and Lady Francis Seymour the children enjoyed tea. The day coincided with Peter Rabbit's 100th birthday, so there was a cake shaped like him, cut by Virginia, Lady Bath. After tea the children were entertained with face painting, magic and juggling.

Mary Ford loved playing with the children and often visited the nursery.

The nursery school in 1995. (Back row) Sam Dufosee, Adam Yeo, Ben Pritchard, Amanda Garton, Daniel Coombs, Judith Frapwell, Ned Scanlon and Daniel Woodland. (Kneeling) Jonathan Haggerty, Robert Ashwell and Christopher Haggerty. (Front) Lottie Lobb, Louise Poolman, Georgina Pollard and Fiona Trimby.

The staff in 1995. Mrs. Wadsworth liked to involve the village in the life of the school, hence the two classroom helpers. The increasing amount of paperwork faced by all schools meant that two administrative assistants were also needed. Standing are Jenny Hines (classroom assistant), Margaret Crossman (secretarial assistant) and Mrs. Fewell (classroom assistant). Seated are Suzanne Carver (infant teacher), Alison Wadsworth (headmistress), Carolyn Spruce (infant teacher) and Jan Pattison (administrative assistant).

School in 1996. The school's success and the subjects it offered were attracting pupils from outside the village. Twenty additional pupils had arrived in the last three years. (Back row) Louisa Daniels, Oliver Moore, Jules Golding, Christina Earle, Leon Widdows, Amy Crossman, Mayra Diaz, Michelle Trollope, Karl Widdows, David Crossman and Edward Earle. (Second row) Alice Trimby, Jack Opie, Amy Hall, Charlotte Bronson, Alice Woods, Max Buston, Jack Crossman, Sam Mason, Liam Howlett, Louise Stevens and Ryan Widdows. (Third row) Philip Allard, Ben Ashley, Matthew Crossman, Max Flewitt, Kirsty Yeo, Polly Elliot-Pyle, Scarlett Garton, David Pritchard, David Trollope and Emma Trollope. (Fourth row) Pippa Harris, Michelle Turney, Fiona Eggleton, Suzanne Carver, Alison Wadsworth, Carolyn Spruce, Felicity Window, Andrew Evans and Natasha Golding. (Fifth row) Toby Mason, Gemma Coombs, Daniel Coombs, Eban Bainbridge, Andrew Window, Lucy Richardson, Ned Scanlon, Daniel Woodland, Christopher Haggerty, Jonathan Haggerty and Georgina Moore. (Front row) Tim Ashley, Sam Dufosee, Jessie Wood and Adam Yeo.

Mrs. Wadsworth's retirement 1996. A party was held in the village hall, at which Mrs. Wadsworth was presented with a wooden garden sun lounger and a Portmeirion fruit bowl. Among the children are Sam Mason, Ryan Widdows, Jack Opie, Pippa Harris and Michelle Trollope.

Mrs. Ivey takes her class in 1998.

Information Technology suite 1998. This was the first set of computers bought for the school and given a specific area in the Hall. Working at them are (l-r) Laura Rolfe, Ryan Widdows, Jack Crossman, Louise Stevens, Sam Mason and Andrew Window.

Reception classroom 1998. The school attracted pupils from outside the village and consequently outgrew itself. The County Council suggested sending pupils elsewhere, but the community chose to help itself by rescuing an old portable classroom from Kingdown School in Warminster. With the help of generous donations and many hours of work by parents over a year the classroom was officially opened by Lord Bath on May 1st. Around the table (l-r) are Georgina Symes, Louis O'Sullivan, Joseph Dufosee and Chelsea Penny.

The 1998 Reunion. The theme for this year was the school, and it was a great success. All day long the school was full of past pupils re-living their time there. This picture shows a group of Mrs. Ivey's pupils who spent the day showing visitors around.

The school from the playground 1998. Victorian schools were built with high windows to prevent the children looking out. They were also the perfect vantage point for Mr. Booker to keep an eye on everyone during lunchtime. His furious hammering on the window pane was enough to stop anyone misbehaving immediately!

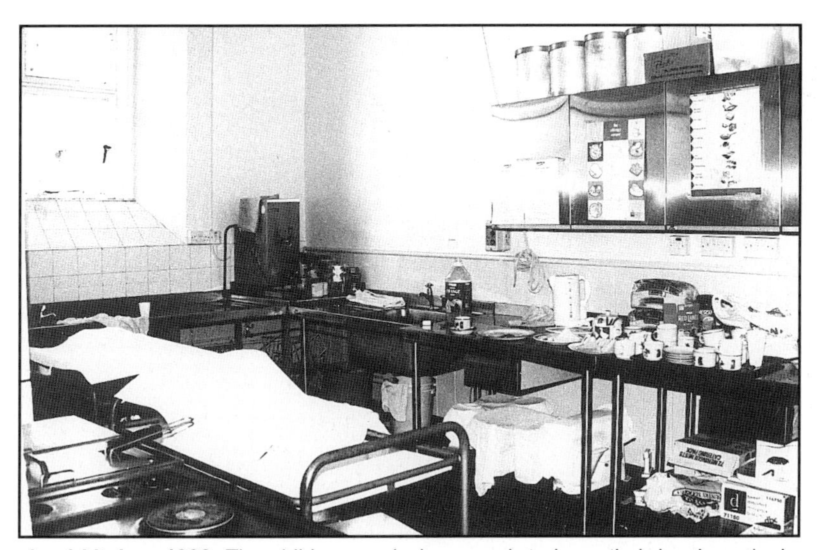

The school kitchen 1998. The children are lucky enough to have their lunch cooked on the premises. I remember enjoying them, and the rush there was for second and third helpings! Mrs. Wadsworth remembers that Friday was roast beef day, and her first job in the morning was to put the oven on. By 11 o'clock the smell of roasting beef made everyone feel hungry.

Christmas party at Longleat 1998. Each year the children attend a party given by Lord Bath at Longleat House. Tea is followed by an entertainment, and then everyone receives a present from Father Christmas. Here the Marquess is handing out toys to Adam Yeo and Daniel Woodland.

Football 1999. The players are Kirsty Yeo, David Trollope, Liam Howlett, Simon Rolfe, Ryan Widdows, Sam Mason. (Front row) Sam Dufosee, Tim Ashley, Andrew Window and Jack Crossman. The coach is parent Gary Dolby.

The school in 1999. (Back row) Ryan Widdows, Emma Trollope, Liam Howlett, Anna Robinson, Kirsty Yeo, Pippa Harris, David Trollope, Simon Rolfe, Jack Crossman, Paul Andrews and Sam Mason. (Second row) Karen Crossman, Tim Ashley, Adam Yeo, Shaun Daniels, Alistair Stride, Louise Stevens, Ned Scanlon, Laura Rolfe, Daniel Woodland, Toby Mason, Sam Dufosee and Robert Ashwell. (Third row) Sophie Richardson, Chelsea Penny, Lieff Milner-Cristo, Jodie Windess, Natalie Stride, Ruth Mullender, Finn Gunning, Luke Hood, Eleanor Grugeon, Vicky Hill and Chantelle Daniels. (Fourth row) Megan Hill, Joe Dufosee, Gedeon Milner-Cristo, Thomas Dolby, Louise Poolman, Joshua Maynard, Lottie Lobb, Louis O'Sullivan, Callum Widdows, Katy Newman, Henry Beaumont and Thomas O'Connor. (Staff) Sue Priestner, Victoria Griffiths, Jenny Hines, Carolyn Spruce, Sue Ivey, Suzanne Carver, Sian Millier, Jan Pattison and Heather Ashley. (Front) Bryony Windess, Wulfric Sainsbury, Robert Grugeon, Ryan Woollaston, Fraser Richardson, Stephanie Ashwell, Charlotte Radley and Ben White.

At Work

In the 19th century most men were labourers, either on farms or in the woods. In 1850 Thomas Pope alone employed 50 men on his 800 acre farm. Until 1940 the land was the main source of employment, numbers declined as machinery was introduced and farmers were forced to cut their labour to meet falling prices. In the 1920s Horningsham had numerous small farms. Mechanical equipment would have been neither necessary nor affordable, and it was only the larger farmer who could take advantage of this new technology. Even by 1954 there were still a quarter of a million horses working in England and Wales.(Longleat Forestry did not buy its first mechanical equipment until c. 1950). Everyone, however, was affected by the financial climate. Ernie Trollope, for example, went bankrupt at Church Farm. From 1940 all the small farmers in the village gradually disappeared. Today there are only five farms in the parish; Mill Farm, Parsonage Farm, Lower Barn, Round Hill and Baycliffe.

Forestry has always been a major interest of the Thynnes. The 1st Marquess of Bath was particularly interested and by his death in 1796 over a million trees had been planted. The work was seasonal and during the winter provided work for every labourer in the area. After the Second World War the forestry department was the main employer and as recently as 1950 employed up to 100 men. However, costs escalated in the 1990s and in 1999 the timber yard was sold to an outside company.

Horningsham was self-sufficient until c. 1939, as it had all the necessary cottage industries. In 1885 we had six shopkeepers, five bootmakers, four beer retailers and other trades such as bakers, carriers, blacksmiths and tailors. Often a man would do several jobs to make ends meet. George Beauchamp was a farmer, thatcher and beer retailer. Joe Curtis worked in the woods but also kept a smallholding - no doubt there were many others like him. Gradually, as people had easier access to the towns and mechanisation improved, these small businesses folded as they were unable to compete. Today, apart from the pub and bed and breakfast at Mill Farm, there is just the one shop in Chapel Street. Thankfully it is still open for business, but in the last ten years numerous proprietors have found it very difficult to make a profit.

When the 5th Marquess of Bath died in 1946 his son was faced with some difficult decisions. The £700,000 bill for death duties had to be paid and after eight years occupation by the Royal School the House was badly in need of renovation. The days of the large domestic household were gone and a family of six did not need a house with 118 rooms. The new Marquess was determined to preserve his home; when his sisters opened it for a day in aid of charity, the response encouraged him to open to the public as a commercial enterprise. The rest, as they say, is history. During the last fifty years the success of the House, and later the Safari Park, has meant that the tourist industry has become the main source of employment. The house, gardens, park, attractions and animals all require staff to look after them. From farm labourer to elephant keeper, from house servant to guide, the changes in the last one hundred years have been immense.

25 Years service awards. The awards were first made in 1971. Lord Weymouth felt that it was appropriate to acknowledge the loyalty of long serving members of staff, noting that the men often worked outside and in bad weather. The twenty men received engraved watches and the two women crystal vases. The wives also received glassware. In the picture, from the back, are Francis Ford, George Welchman (Cheddar), Billy Rowe, George Mathews, Eric Mathews, Frank Eggleton, Jim Dix, Victor Trollope, Walt Clark, Edgar Churchill, Harold Doman, Bill Potter, Les Hardiman, Fred Curtis, Wally Trollope, Roy Trollope, Bill Roberts, Jim Ford, Lionel Marsh, Sybil Watts and Ernie Berry. Seated are Lily McClurg, Lord and Lady Bath and Lord Weymouth.

Longleat House Cleaners. When the House first opened to the public there were eight cleaners; now there are only four. Pictured right are Mary Hoddinott, Mary Dix, Frances Trollope, Pam Carpenter and Katie Capp. The ladies on the left, June Windess, Marie Clarke and Barbara Bond were photographed shortly before the screening of the Lion Country television series in 1998. They had cleaned the House for between seventeen and twenty one years. Cleaning seventeen rooms each day the team used 108 tins of brass polish and 120 dusters each every year.

Moving the State Coach. The family Coach, built by Barkers of London c. 1750, has been used at every coronation since that of George IV in 1821. The coach and livery are in the family colours of black and gold. Its last outing was in the procession of the Lord Mayor of London in 1964. When these pictures were taken the coach was kept at the bottom of the Grand Staircase in Longleat House. Occasionally it had to be moved, which meant dismantling it and taking it out through the front doors piece by piece. In the pictures are George Mathews, Errol Williams, Paddy Dalton, Ian Windel, Tony Moy and David Forest.

Café Staff in 1953. Longleat House opened to the public in 1949 and the cellars were converted into a café in 1951. In the picture from the back are Mr. Chapman, Mrs. Marsh, Mrs. Chapman, Mrs. Garth, Mrs. Dix, Mrs. Barnes, Mrs. Seymour, Mrs. Robertson, Mrs. McClurg and Master Garth.

The stableyard, Longleat. Pictured are ? , Alfie Marsh, George Mathews and Alan Keyse. When George left school in 1935 he became an apprentice carpenter on the estate. After the war he returned as an improver and went on to work for 35 years maintaining Longleat House.

Topiary trimming at Longleat. Head Gardener Fred Chapman tries out a mechanical hedge trimmer in the 1950s. Les Wheeler looks on.

Heaven's Gate. Until c. 1970 Lord Bath charged visitors to the estate on summer evenings. Bert Dredge is collecting the toll.

Three groundsmen in 1999. These three men have all worked on the estate for over 30 years. Graham Eggleton has worked 33 years. Gordon Taylor started in the forestry and has worked 40 years. Victor Trollope also spent most of his time in the forestry and is the longest serving member of staff on the whole estate with 53 years service.

Storm at Shearwater, 1910. These men are clearing trees that blew down in a bad storm in February 1910. Harry Rowe is in the foreground.

Moving the State Coach. Jack Marsh and George Trollope with horses Major and Boxer.

Lord Bath and Reg Guy (forestry foreman) are just visible standing beneath these massive trees. This photo was taken in 1947 at Gamblers Clump, Gypsy Lane (near Bradley Road, Warminster). The trees, planted in 1875, are Douglas Fir, Norway Spruce and Californian Redwoods.

Shearwater Sawmill. During the First World War the ladies helped out at the timber yard. The planking they are sitting on was used to construct the camps on Salisbury Plain. It would be nice to put some names to these faces.

Forestry Stables. Pictured at the stables near Forest House are Jack Marsh, Bert Dredge and Sid Hawkins. The working day started at 7am, feeding, grooming and harnessing the horses. The walk to the woods began at 8am, taking almost two hours to walk to Southleigh Woods, for example. Arriving in time for the mid-morning meal break meant that timber work did not begin until 10.30am. The horses needed new shoes once a month, and went to the smith at Maiden Bradley on a Saturday morning. Mr. Wheeler eventually bought a horse box to shorten the journey time to the woods. One morning, as it was travelling down Church Street, the base fell out of the box leaving the horses feet sticking out of the bottom! No doubt they walked to work that day!

Loading timber. After the war Longleat bought two David Brown tractors to help transport the timber. During the war these tractors were used to move aircraft and bomb trailers around the airfields. After the war they were sold. Roy Trollope steadies the tree trunk as the tractor winches it onto the trailer.

Taking timber to Gloucester. Two Goodyear representatives pose with Les Wheeler. These trees were bought by a firm in Gloucestershire. Travelling at an average of ten miles an hour, this load would have taken Stan Doel approximately five hours to deliver.

Frome Show. In the 1950s Les Wheeler had a stand at Frome Show for the forestry department. A small crowd watches a demonstration of making stakes. Stan Doel is at the front of the stand.

Four woodsmen, possibly at Norridge Woods. L-r Bert Dredge, Bill Roberts, Jim Dix and Charlie Carpenter.

Charcoal burning. Victor Trollope stands by the kiln at Norridge Woods c. 1950. This was a skill that went back to the 16th century, as charcoal was a vital ingredient in the manufacture of iron. It burns at very high temperatures relative to wood, and so made iron-smelting possible. It was later used as an industrial filter and to make artists materials, but by the 1980s the craft had almost died out. The skill lies in loading the timber carefully and sealing the kiln at the right moment, otherwise the wood will burn rather than carbonise. A skilled man could turn two and a half tons of wood into seven hundredweight of charcoal.

Preparing the timber. Victor Trollope, Sid Carpenter, Roy Trollope and George Hill cut the wood into four foot lengths ready for the kiln.

The kiln at Hog's Back. There was a second kiln at Longleat, where the lion reserve now is. Keeper Frank Doel is pictured with George Hill and Ted Marsh.

King's Bottom, Longhedge, Corsley. The forestry foreman, Rodney Garton and the head forester John McHardy in 1999.

Ernest Robertson feeds the turkeys and chickens at Stalls Farm in the 1920s. In the background is a thatched haystack.

Joe Curtis. Joe and his family lived at Newbury. He served in India during the First World War. Many years later he enjoyed telling his grand daughter tales about his time there. She remembers that every morning grandpa had to tip his boots upside down before putting them on, to make sure there were no scorpions in them! On his return Joe worked in the woods with the horses, but he also kept a smallholding. Unfortunately he lost all his pigs to swine fever, after which he kept poultry instead. Joe took over the farm at Newbury from Arthur Adlam, hence the name on the cart.

Church Farm c. 1935. Ernest Trollope farmed Church Farm from 1932-1938. The boy in the pictures is Eddie Ball, who worked for Mr. Trollope.

Bakery Farm, Chapel Street. This was a grocer's and a bakery as early as 1850, when James Trollope was the grocer and master baker. In 1890 it passed to George Chapman and has been in that family ever since. George also kept pigs and cured the bacon. His son Edward ran the farm and a small shop until the early 1940s when he retired and swopped houses with his son Arthur, who also lived in Chapel St. Arthur and his wife Jessie ran the shop until the 1960s and the farm until 1969. When Jessie died in 1999 their son Roy moved into the family home.

Mr. and Mrs. Arthur Russell at Lower Barn Farm in 1941. These soldiers were stationed at Sutton Veny camp for their initial training. As Mr. Russell was short of labour, they helped to bring in the harvest. Apparently harvesting was preferable to square bashing!

Wheat in stooks, Parsonage Farm in 1957. On a fine August day these acres of perfect wheat are always a beautiful sight. Today Mr. Whatley sells his crop for seed. At every harvest festival he gives the church two sheaves and two sacks of corn, a tradition that reminds us that although harvesting methods change, the village still comes together to give thanks each year for the crops we have gathered.

Parsonage Farm, 1957. Bill Whatley, who came to Horningsham in 1949, was the first farmer in the village to make silage. His four year old twins John and Judy stand by the Italian ryegrass to show how high it was. These large fields were the parish glebe lands for many centuries.

The village shop. John Hulbert and his wife pose outside the shop with their delivery boy Ernest Trollope. They ran the stores together from 1892-1924. In the window on the left is a parrot cage, the bird was used to alert the shopkeeper when a customer arrived. Mr. Hulbert also ran a bakery within the shop. The sheds opposite the stores were the stables for the horses.

Tom Dicks at the shop. Tom worked for Mr. Hulbert, and eventually took over the business in 1929. Molly Dunn (née Carpenter) recalls: 'We had to carry everything we bought which included paraffin. The shop was nothing like it is today. Items such as sugar, rice and fruit were weighed into strong blue paper bags and butter and lard was cut to the size you wanted. We were allowed a ha'penny a week to spend and would search for that wonderful something. You could have five toffees, a sherbet dab, liquorice, sugar mice - so many things we were spoilt for choice. When we paid for the shopping Mr. Dicks would give us a big bag of broken biscuits – what a treat that was and so kind.' The shop was later run by his two sons Douglas and Cyril, remaining in the family until c. 1970.

Above: Model T Ford van. This was purchased by John Hulbert. (His name is just visible on the driver's door.) Tom Dicks is on the right, with Eddie Carpenter his delivery man.

Left: Derrick Robins also delivered for Tom Dicks, but his was a more modest form of transport!

Ivan Haskell and his wife Dorothy took over the shop when Cyril Dicks retired. In 1971 Charlie Barnes retired as sub-postmaster and the Post Office moved into the shop.

Longleat's gamekeepers. In 1919 Peter Stockley, the head gamekeeper, retired. He is in the middle of the front row. Mr. Stockley came to Longleat in 1879 and was in charge of an estate of 30,000 acres, 5,000 of which were woodland. The annual bag of pheasants regularly reached 10,000 and not one egg was bought. When the Prince of Wales (later King Edward VII) visited Longleat 3,433 pheasants were shot in four days. In the picture, from the back, are James Sims, James Watts, Stewart Stockley, John Hale. Frederick Beale, Frederick Carrier, Henry Lewer, Charles Lucas, William Bell. Isaac Garrett, Edward Parker, Richard Futcher, Peter Stockley, Frederick Mussell, Abraham Garrett and Charles Barter.

A shoot in 1965. The Marquess of Bath let the shooting on his 4,000 acres to a building tycoon Mr. F.G. Minter. In the picture, taken at Pottle St, are (l-r) Michael Batley (assistant keeper), Fred Minter, ?, ?, Monty Penny, ?, Major Goldsberry, Mr. Alan and Monty Penny jnr. Mr. Penny, the youngest of four sons of a gamekeeper, started by working for his father before he left school. He came to Longleat from Essex, where he was already working for Mr. Minter, in 1964. On an average day Mr. Penny covered twenty miles patrolling the estate. The birds were fed, the shoot planned and a constant look out kept for vermin.

Beaters at Pottle Street. Preparing for a day's beating are (l-r) Bill Faulkner, Billy Rowe, Sandy Trollope, Les Hardiman, ? and Wally Trollope. The men were each paid 35s for the day.

Esme Battson carries water from the pump on the Common to her home at 138 West Common, c. 1927.

Sid Carpenter trims the verges in Church Lane with a reap hook. Sid started work in the forestry department and was later employed by the council to keep the village verges tidy. For many years he worked alongside Ernie Stevens. The picture was taken in 1979 by the schoolmaster Tim Hill, who had a go himself but found the job difficult. The reap hook is a sharp and efficient tool in skilled hands. It is now a thing of the past, its place having been taken by the strimmer.

Thatching at West Common, 1977. Many of the thatched cottages in the village now have tiled roofs, but there are still a number that have managed to retain this traditional roofing material. As a roof is only thatched once every twenty years or so, the school children were taken along to watch. They followed the progress of the work as a project.

Leathers Coaches. In 1998 the last Leathers coach took passengers from Maiden Bradley and Horningsham to Warminster. After 78 years of service the owners finally retired. Both Don Newbury and Len Cooper started working for the company in the 1920s driving a horse-and-cart. They are pictured with Horningsham passengers Brian Trollope and Mary Ford.

Staff at the Bath Arms. In the back row are Lottie Barnes(left) and Florrie Phillips (right). In the foreground is Ernie Trollope. Does anyone know the others?

Horningsham Home Guard. From the back, they are: Dennis Howlett, Arthur Ford, Maurice Robertson, Ernest Robertson, Roy Trollope, Wally Trollope, ?, Donald Marsh, Jeff Hoddinott. (Middle) Francis Ford, Bob Maggs, Eddie Carpenter, Cyril Dicks, Jack Allard, Jacob Dicks, Lewis Dredge, Sam Garrett, ? Rowe, Albert Moody, Jack Pearce, Stan Ford, ? Hinks, ? Chalk. (Front) Frank Barnes, Bill Marsh, Walt Pullen, Fred Chapman, ? Pincombe, ? Cox, Lewis Marsh, Alfie Marsh, Charlie Barnes, ?, Percy Edwards.

Warminster Police Division c. 1910. Longleat and Horningsham had their own officer, William James (middle row, third right). There was also an officer stationed permanently at Longleat House, Francis Breach (front row, first right).

People

Every community needs it leaders: people who not only want to be involved in village activities but who are willing to organise and run them. Seventy years ago people looked to those in positions of authority to lead them. The vicar, churchwardens, schoolteachers, school managers, doctor, policeman, head forester and head gardener were all important members of the community.

There is also the importance of continuity. Some Horningsham families can be traced back to Sir John Thynne's time. Trollope, Marsh, Thorne, Ford, Carpenter, Adlam and Chapman are all names from the 16th century. These families had a sense of loyalty, not only to their employer but also their community and felt it was their duty to be involved in all aspects of the community.

Life today is very different. Families no longer stay in the same place for generation after generation, sometimes because they cannot afford to do so. Television and video mean that a lot of us stay at home for our entertainment.We all lead busy lives and do not have the time to devote to village activities. The church, chapel, school and hall are important to the life of our community. Let us hope that there will always be people who believe this and who will continue to breathe life into them all.

Thomas Davis snr. was steward to the 1st and 2nd Marquess of Bath. He came to Longleat as a clerk aged 14 in 1763, rising to the post of steward in 1779. He was still in post when he died in 1807. Together with the 1st Marquess he was responsible for extensive improvements to the quality of Longleat's farmland and livestock. A revolution in farming methods was taking place, transforming English agriculture, and the two men did all they could to keep pace with this. In 1794 Davis published the agricultural survey of Wiltshire.

Dr. James Bothwell. Dr. Bothwell was born in Ireland in 1858 and came to Horningsham twenty years later. He was the village doctor and dentist until he died in 1928. He was very popular with the villagers, and for many years was a churchwarden and school manager.

Three generations of the Robins family c. 1915. This was taken outside 137 Broadslade, the home of William Robins and his wife Laura. She is holding her son Derrick, and with her is her mother Laura Ford.

Nellie Trollope's wedding in 1916. The family pose for a photograph outside their home, 90 Water Lane. Nellie married William People, whom she met while she was in service. Also in the picture are her parents Tom and Amelia, brothers Arthur and Ernest, and sisters Annie, Lucy, Lizzie, Frances and Chrissie.

Frank Garrett and Albert Honey outside 54 White St c. 1940. Albert came to Horningsham as an evacuee in 1939. His mother and younger brother were already evacuated to Somerset. By chance, Albert and his father visited this Somerset family on the same day as Frank and Ethel Garrett, who volunteered to look after him for the duration. He was very happy with them, and has many fond memories of Horningsham. Albert clearly remembers his first evening in his new home, asking why the houses had 'straw hats', and being fascinated by the oil lamps. After the war Albert returned to London, but he always spent part of his summer holiday with the Garretts. He visited Frank every year until he died in 1978, and still enjoys coming to the village with his wife and family.

Ernest Chapman, Ray Garrett and Harold Howlett home on leave in 1943. Ernest and Harold were in the navy and Ray worked in the mines.

The wedding of Ray and Olive New in 1944. Olive was a WAAF teleprinter operator based at Longleat and Ray was an artillery officer. They were married at Horningsham a fortnight before D-Day. This wedding is special because Olive wore the first Roosevelt dress. Eleanor Roosevelt, wife of the President of the USA, lent, along with her society friends, a collection of wedding gowns for girls in Britain to use. Each bride paid 10s to have the dress cleaned at the end of the ceremony and then passed it on to someone else.

Mr. and Mrs. Fred Chapman. Fred was born in 1891, and lived at the Lodge for most of his life. He left school at 12 and worked in the gardens at Longleat. He spent a short time working in Scotland for the Duke of Roxburgh, and then served in France during World War One. After the war he returned to Longleat gardens and stayed until 1974. During World War Two Fred was a Quartermaster in the Home Guard. He played football and cricket for the village. He and his wife worshipped at the Chapel where Fred was Senior Deacon. He was a keen gardener and served on the Flower Show Committee. Mabel was born in Oxfordshire in 1896, and came to Longleat House to work in 1917. She was a founder of the Chapel Women's Guild and its secretary for 39 years. She was also a member of the Women's Institute and the Darby and Joan Club, and news correspondent to all the local papers for 20 years.

The retirement of Leslie Wheeler in 1960. Mr. Wheeler was head forester at Longleat from 1945 and chairman of the Parish Council from 1950. He was also responsible for the highly successful pantomimes put on by the Horningsham Revellers, writing and producing them from 1948-1954. This picture shows the presentation to Mr. and Mrs. Wheeler by the Parish Council. Pictured from the back are Francis Ford, Arthur Ford, Rev. Archie Kew, John Crossman, Fred Chapman, Charlie Barnes, Douglas Dicks, Reg Robbins, Mrs. Allard, Catherine Dicks, Walt Clark, Les Wheeler, Doris Wheeler, Janet Whatley and Miss Anderson.

The Crossman family at Mill Farm c. 1980. John and Vera took over Mill Farm in 1954. It was a dairy farm until 1974, since when it has been a mixed farm of cattle, sheep and arable. In 1966 Vera and Valerie Wheeler opened Tea Rooms at the farm and in 1976 Vera started bed and breakfast. In 1970 afternoon tea would have cost you 25p, and a farmhouse tea 29p. A cheese sandwich was 9p and a pot of tea 7p. How prices have changed in 30 years! John and Vera retired in 1997 and their son Stephen took over the farm. The picture shows John and Vera with their children Stephen, Jacqueline and Peter.

Francis Ford MBE. Francis was born in Horningsham in 1915 and except for service in the RAF during the war has lived in the village all his life. His first job on leaving school was at Stourhead. He has also worked at Church Farm in Horningsham, the Warminster Timber Company and Longleat forestry. Francis is a great supporter of village activities. In 1999 he retired from four committees after almost 50 years service - the Parish Council, the Parochial Church Council, the Village Hall and Village Fayre. He was both secretary and treasurer of the Hall. This service was rewarded in 1993 when Francis was presented with the MBE by the Lord Lieutenant of Wiltshire at a party at the Hall.

The War Memorial. This was unveiled in 1920. Horningsham lost 24 men in the First World War, 4% of the population. In such a small community everyone would have been affected by this loss. One cannot begin to imagine how a young man who had spent all his life in a Wiltshire village would have felt when faced with the horrors of the battlefield. The next generation were also severely affected - only four men were lost in the Second World War.

Remembrance Sunday in 1999. Every year the villagers gather to remember the fallen. A communion service at the church is followed by a short service at the Memorial. Pictured here after the service are Canon Roger Sharpe, the Rev. and Mrs. Yates, Mr. Morgan, Mr. and Mrs. Hines, Mr. and Mrs. Crossman and Miss Douglas-Pennant.

Recreation

Reading through the *Warminster Journals*, it soon became clear to me that there were a lot of recreational activities in Horningsham between 1900 and 1960. Fortunately there were people willing to set up and run various groups, and the villagers always supported all that went on. Admittedly the only entertainment available was that organised by the residents for themselves, but there was also a strong community spirit that made people want to support events.

Groups were centred around the church, chapel, school, the hall and before that the reading room. At the church you could join the choir, the PCC or the Mothers Union. The chapel had a Womens Guild. The schoolmaster, Mr. Welborn, was very musical and would often give concerts in the schoolroom. The reading room had newspapers, magazines and books, billiards and other games. The hall was the home of the Womens Institute, the youth club and the pantomime. Sport was represented by football, cricket and bowls. There were also annual events such as the school treat and the flower show.

Sadly, times have changed and so has the community. We all have a large number of activities to choose from and less time to do them. There are also fewer people willing to put time and effort into running these activities. Some have survived longer than others. The football team, founded in 1902, still plays. Cricket folded in 1999 after more than a hundred years. The Womens Institute also folded in the same year after 79 years. It would be nice to think that one day they will be revived.

Motor meet at Longleat 1906. The Motor Union of Great Britain held a meeting at Bath and a large number of the finest cars in England attended. In the afternoon the cars left for Longleat, where, by the invitation of the Marquess of Bath, a hill climbing competition, organised by the Somerset Automobile Club, took place. The measured distance extended from the bridge near Longleat House, over Heaven's Gate to Dod Pool, and formed one of the best hill climbing tests to be found in the locality.

Gymkhana (?). Little is known about this picture. It appears to be a gymkhana or other sporting event. The location is a field at Broadslade. There is a note on the back suggesting that the little boy in the foreground facing the camera is Harry Dicks. The man three to the right of Harry may be Alexander Cameron.

The Hunt c. 1910. Probably the South and West Wilts Hunt, at a meet outside the Bath Arms.

The village hut. The present Village Hall was built in 1930 by the Marquess of Bath in memory of his wife. Before this there was a tin hut on the site. The lady on the left is Lottie Dicks and on the right is Floss Trollope.

Charabanc outing to Cheddar c. 1920. Mr. and Mrs. Fred Humphries are sitting next to the driver. The little girl in the white hat with the cave notice behind her is Ivy Found. Note the solid tyres and acetylene lamps.

Outing to Southampton.

Another outing. Again, Fred Humphries is next to the same driver as at Cheddar. Standing next to him with a cigarette is Frank Dredge. The vehicle now has pneumatic tyres and electric lamps.

W.I. outing to Bournemouth 1928. Miss Anderson and Miss Windo are standing in the centre in front of the white sign. The charabanc now has side curtains.

The Hall swings c. 1927. Floss Trollope with Kathleen and Esme Battson. The swings look very sturdy, but Sidney Battson confesses that his family were responsible for breaking them!

Tree planting in 1937. Joshua Dicks, the oldest village native, planted a tree at the Village Hall to commemorate the coronation of George VI.

Swedish scouts. In 1959 a group of Swedish scouts visited England. They spent a day at Longleat, where they were the guests of the 1st Horningsham Cubs. Cub mistress Mrs. Foster is in the centre of the picture. The District Commissioner, the Rev. Biddlecombe from Chitterne is seated on her left.

The Harvest auction. When Ernie Trollope was landlord at the Bath Arms, the produce given to the church Harvest Festival was auctioned in the café behind the pub. The auction later transferred to the Hall for many years, but has now returned to the pub. The produce has changed little over the years, a good mixture of flowers, fresh food, tins and corn. Unfortunately I have never seen a crate of beer!

Flower Show race, 1912. Eight men line up for the mile race, which was started by Mr. Cameron. The winner was C.H. Worsdell from Warminster. Second and third came from Chippenham and Melksham. Sandy Trollope is the gentleman in the middle wearing collar and tie.

Flower Show princess. In 1952 the princess was Sylvia Warn, seen here with her attendants Ann Wheeler and Vera Trollope.

Flower Show c. 1953. Among those trying their luck on Arthur Ford's spinning arrow are Tommy Eggleton and Gordon Taylor.

Flower Show. In 1955 the Show moved from the Hall to the Bath Arms. Ernie Trollope was well known for his superb dahlias, which people would travel miles to see. Admiring the exhibits with him are Miss Anderson and Mrs. Foster.

The Horningsham Revellers. Between 1948 and 1955 Leslie Wheeler wrote and produced an annual pantomime in the village. Lots of people were involved, either acting or backstage, and they all had a lot of fun. The 1951 production was Robinson Crusoe.

Cinderella in 1952. The cast included Joan Edwards, Merigon Dufosee, Sylvia Berry, Susan Barnes, Valerie Taylor, Jim, Mary and Jimmy Ford, Florence Barnes, Ken and Muriel Doel, William Garrett, Douglas Dicks, Francis Ford, Ann Wheeler, Kathleen Barnes, Vera Trollope, Kathleen Alford, Hester Rowe, Margaret Eggleton, Glenys Evans, Janet Dredge, David Taylor, Ben Dufosee and Doris Wheeler. The musicians were Islay Peet and Arthur Ford.

Darby and Joan Club. This group was inspired by the Warminster WVS, and held its first meeting in March 1952. The members enjoyed playing whist and table croquet, reading, and a raffle and refreshments. Enjoying afternoon tea on an outing are Mrs. Rowe, Mrs. Barnes, Margaret Barrett, Mrs. Reynolds, Mrs. Barrett, Mr. and Mrs. Farrer, Mr. and Mrs. Jarvis, Jacob Dicks, Mr. and Mrs. Churchill, Don Newbury, Mrs. Goring, Mrs. Crosby, Mrs. Foakes and Mrs. Curtis.

W.I. Anniversary. This party was probably celebrating the W.I.'s 30th anniversary in 1949. The ladies are Mesdames Clark, Gould, Doel, Hunt, Carpenter, Barter, Wheeler, Garrett, Evans, Seymour, Dredge, Dix, Chapman, Edwards, Long, Price, Robbins, Reynolds, Curtis, Churchill, Peet, Davis, Marsh, Lady Bath, Barnes, Ridout, Doman, Woodey, Long, Barnes, Ford, Grey, Barnes, Whatley, Trollope and Dicks.

Tree planting ceremony. The W.I. presented a tree to Lord Bath c. 1964 which was planted in the pets cemetery. Susan Bowen wields the spade. Also pictured are Margaret Barrett, Lottie Barnes, Mary Dix, Mrs. Edgar Curtis, Leonie Taylor, Pam Carpenter, Doreen Dearman, Doris Long, Helen Riley, Veronica Clark, Joyce Clark, Florence Carpenter and Dora Larkin.

W.I. play rehearsal. In 1963 the newly-formed W.I. Drama Group presented their first full length play, 'Ladies in Waiting'. It was produced by Susan Bowen, a professional performer who appeared many times on BBC television and radio. The budding actresses are Edith Carter, Vera Crossman, Valerie Wheeler, Doris Long, Dorothy Webb, Pat Osborne, Margaret Eggleton, Doreen Clark, Leonie Taylor and Susan Bowen.

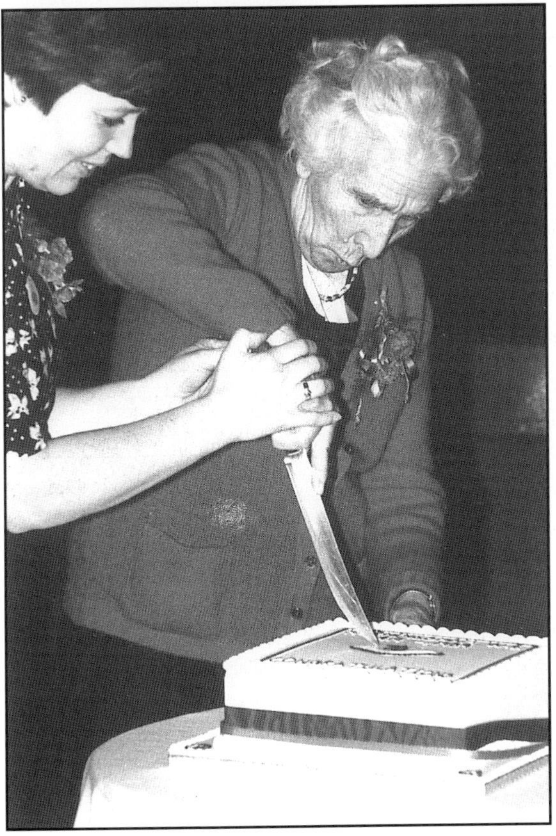

W.I. 70th birthday. The W.I. was founded in 1919 and continued until 1999 when it sadly folded due to a decline in membership numbers. Miss Anderson and Suzanne Carver cut the cake. Other members are Ann Trollope, Hazel Gillingham, Joyce Lovelock, Anthea Doman, Vera Lee, Doris Harding, Christine Noall, Margaret Crossman, Mary Dix, Anne Davies, Connie Gunner, Jenny Hines, Kathleen Trollope, Pam Perry, Susan Douglas-Pennant, Linda Young, Marion Ashley, Barbara Carpenter, Parri Hooper, Gwen Gillingham, Jill Banks and Mary Ford.

Mothers Union c. 1957. The ladies are pictured at a meeting at Stalls Farm, the home of enrolling member Mrs. Frank Reynolds. In the back row are Mrs. Barrett, Margaret Barrett, ?, ?, Mrs. Dix, ?, Mrs. Mathews, Mrs. Cox, Mrs. Carter and Mrs. Barter. Seated are ?, Mrs. Reynolds, Mrs. Curtis, Mrs. Seymour, ?, Mrs. Barnes, Mrs. Carpenter and Alison Dix (child).

Miss Anderson's retirement. When Miss Anderson retired as headmistress of the school in 1965 a party was held in her honour at the village hall. She was presented with a television set and some rose bushes for her garden. In the picture are Bill, Doris and Margaret Long, Mrs. Meeker, Mrs. Churchill, Andrew Bowen and Neil Carpenter. On the opposite side are ?, Mrs. Whatley, Pauline Long, ?, Mrs. Leslie Long, Mrs. Dyke, ?, Kathleen Long, Mr. and Mrs. Charlie Barnes and Kathleen, George Mathews.

Childrens Christmas tea party c. 1966. Each year the W.I. organised a party for the small children in the village. For many years Miss Anderson chose the presents, keeping a list to make sure no one got the same present twice. The girls often received a doll's cradle made by Mr. Baverstock. Enjoying the tea are Mrs. King with David, Martin and Gordon, Thelma Moore and Adrian, Joan Trollope and Andrew, Leonie Taylor and Helen, Jenny McClurg and Sheila, ?, Stephen Crossman and Andrew Bowen.

Among those under the Christmas tree are Stephen, Peter and Jacqueline Crossman, Andrew Bowen, Peter Clark, Lester Carpenter, Helen Taylor, David King and Christine Baggs.

Lucky numbers quiz. Horningsham entered this television quiz, chaired by Noel Edmonds, c. 1978. They won a park bench, some flower bulbs and wooden litter bins.

Cricket. Village cricket became popular in the late 19th century, and Horningsham's team was founded then. Both cricket and football had a mixture of Horningsham and Longleat players, and the teams used both names. The cricket pitch was at Longleat. In this 1920s picture are (from the back, left to right) M. Dredge, Gilbert Carpenter, Mr. Collins, P. Tinns, ?, Edward Cracknell, E. Curtis, ?, Alexander Cameron, Charlie Davis, ?, D. Curtis, Harry Hillier and Bill Hoddinott.

Cricket in the 1950s. Left to right are Dennis Gooding, Charlie Barnes, ?, Stan Doel, Freddie Curtis, Harold Winslow, C.G. Long, Derrick Robins, Harry Hillier, ?, Mr. Watts.

The Stragglers Cricket Club. This was a Warminster based club formed in 1957. They played only evening matches, usually twenty overs each side. Doug Lakey remembers many a good game played against Horningsham, and there were always excellent refreshments afterwards at the Bath Arms. The annual dinner was also held there. This picture is the 1959 dinner. Ernie Trollope is behind the bar and Walt Clark is in the background. Among the others enjoying a drink are Albert Ayers, Jack Riley, George Kingston, Bill Maidment, Doug Lakey, Dick Voisey, Phillip Moody and Ron Shergold.

Football. The football club was founded in 1902. Among the players in the 1920 team are Fred Chapman, Joe Field, Harry Hillier and Charlie Davis. Mr. Cameron is standing on the right.

Football c. 1955. (Back row l-r) Tony Adlam, Bill Hurd, Roy Mengham, Gordon Taylor, Norman Stanley, ?, John Stay, ?. (Front row) ? Tanner, John Hurd, Alan Mathews and Reg Jones.

Football 1966. (Back row) Tony Doman, Alan Keyse, David Eggleton, Keith Dix, Paddy Berry, Martin Clark, Brian Trollope. (Front row) Robert Penny, Charles Clark, Brian Trim, Tony Mead, Michael Trollope and David Penny.

Football in 1973. This was the year Horningsham won the league cup and the hospital cup. (Back row) Mr. Penny, Eric Gough, Tony Rogers, Mick Ednay, Keith Dix, Brian Pollard. (Front row) David Penny, Chris Martin, Monty Penny, Joe McMann, Robert Penny and Jim Dix.

Skittle Alley. c. 1952 a new skittle alley was opened at the Bath Arms. Lord Bath bowls the first ball. Ernie Trollope and keeper Frank Doel are to the right.

Skittles c. 1970. Pictured are Walt Clark, Edgar Churchill, Harold Doman, Michael Trollope, John Moore, Brian Trollope, Lord and Lady Bath and Joyce Clark.

Skittles c. 1987. The captain was Ginny Pollard, who named her team 'The Gin and It's. This was the year they won the league. The team was Brian Pollard, Pearl Penny, Jenny McClurg, Ginny, ?, Mark Young and Carol Penny.

Hens at the Lodge. Walt Clark moved to the Lodge after getting married in 1944. His garden and his hens were his two favourite hobbies. The hens were a familiar site to walkers in the Pleasure Walk for over 50 years, and people would often stop to look at a hen and her chicks on the lawn. Walt died in 1996. His son Peter still keeps hens, but they have now been moved to his garden across the road.

Above: Best kept village competition. Horningsham has won this three times, in 1978 and 1979 as the best small village, and in 1983 as medium village. Cllr. Alwyn Curtis, chairman of W.W.D.C., presented the award to John Crossman. Mrs. Gladys Shorto, editor of the Warminster Journal, presented the cheque to Lesley Trollope. Lord Margadale is in the background.

Left: In 1983 John Crossman received the award from John Wesley, chairman of W.W.D.C.

The Luncheon Club. The club was started in 1983 by Hazel Gillingham and Brenda Mackintosh. At the first meeting in February seventeen members sat down to beef casserole and apple pie. Mrs. Trollope (below) collected the subscriptions. In 1983 Lord and Lady Bath were guests. They are pictured with Charlie Barnes, Ernie Stevens, Mrs. Williams, Bill Potter, Wally Trollope and Lottie Barnes.

Ploughing match. In 1986 Victor Marsh, who worked for Bill Whatley, won a class in a ploughing match at Corsley, organised by Frome Young Farmers Club.

Tug-of-War team. In 1990 there was a tug-of-war contest at the village fayre between the village and the army. This was an annual event, and the army always won! The team were Clive Eggleton, Ian Blair, John Radley, Carl Trollope, Tony Doman, ?, Andrew Strong, Jeremy Trollope and Steve Davies.

New Year's Eve 1999. I thought it appropriate for the book to end with the very last event in the village in the 20th century. A party was held in the Village Hall, with music provided by Tim Steer and his family. Among those enjoying the music are David and Jenny Hines, David O'Connor, Kate Harris, Carl and Tina Trollope, Keith Shattock, Brian Trollope and David and Ann-Marie Green.